INTERLINK ILLUSTRATED HISTORIES

W9-BFO-117

Gandhi and India

41-49, 120-121
51-80 - 128,129

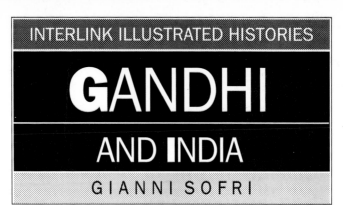

INTERLINK ILLUSTRATED HISTORIES

GANDHI

AND INDIA

GIANNI SOFRI

Translated by Janet Sethre Paxia

INTERLINK BOOKS

An imprint of Interlink Publishing Group, Inc.

New York

First American edition published in 1999 by

INTERLINK BOOKS
An imprint of Interlink Publishing Group, Inc.
99 Seventh Avenue · Brooklyn, New York 11215 and
46 Crosby Street · Northampton, Massachusetts 01060

Library of Congress Cataloging-in-Publication Data
Sofri, Gianni.
    [Gandhi e L'India. English]
    Gandhi and India / Gianni Sofri : translated by Janet Sethre Paxia.
        p. cm. — (Interlink illustrated histories)
    Includes bibliographical references and index.
    ISBN 1-56656-239-2
    1. Gandhi, Mahatma, 1869-1948—Political and social views.
    2. India—Politics and government—1919-1947. 3. India—
    History—20th century. I. Title. II. Series.
    DS481.G3S574313   1999
    954.035092–dc21   98-20062
                                                          CIP

Typeset by Archetype IT Ltd., website: www.archetype-it.com
Printed and bound in Italy

To order or request our complete catalog,
please call us at **1-800-238-LINK** or write to:
Interlink Publishing
46 Crosby Street, Northampton, MA 01060
e-mail: interpg@aol.com • website: www.interlinkbooks.com

Contents

GANDHI AND INDIA

For a long time, people have argued over Gandhi's importance as a universal figure. Can his experience have relevance elsewhere? Or must one emphasize, above all else, his Indianness, the particular nature of his tradition and culture? Actually, the two aspects are not contradictory, as we shall see in the course of this book. An Indian by birth and by some of the traditions he embraced, Gandhi's legacy nonetheless belongs to all the peoples of the earth. We shall see, among other things, how elements of the Indian tradition are closely interwoven in his thought with those of Western origin: it is significant that a Russian, Tolstoy; an Englishman, Ruskin; and an American, Thoreau, were his favorite authors. At the same time, it would be difficult to understand Gandhi if we isolated him from his geographical, historical, and cultural context. So we must, indeed, make this context our starting point.

Chapter 1

THE INDIAN WORLD:
AN INTRODUCTION

FOR FOUR THOUSAND YEARS A MOSAIC OF DRAMATIC
CONTACTS AND CONTRASTS AMONG DIFFERENT CULTURES, THE
INDIAN SUBCONTINENT MET UP WITH EUROPEAN COLONIALISM
IN THE EIGHTEENTH AND NINETEENTH CENTURIES.
CONFRONTATION WITH BRITISH DOMINATION SET THE STAGE
FOR THE BIRTH OF A NATION.

To begin with, what do we mean when we speak of "India?" The question seems banal, but it is less so than one might think. India is, first of all, a vast geographic area (a "subcontinent," as it is often called), stretching over an area just over one-third the size of the United States and more than twelve times larger than the United Kingdom. But India is also a nation, which has been independent since 1947. It is second only to China in number of inhabitants, and seventh in the world in size (after Russia, Canada, China, United States, Brazil, and Australia). Today, other independent nations occupy the Indian subcontinent alongside India: Pakistan, Nepal, Bhutan, Bangladesh, and Sri Lanka. Afghanistan, to the northwest, and Burma (today Myanmar) to the northeast, function in a sense as gateways to the subcontinent. Through them it looks out toward the world of Central Asia, on one hand, and the world of Southeast Asia, on the other. Further contacts have taken place, over the centuries, by way of the sea: on one side, the Indian Ocean joins the island of Sri Lanka and the Deccan coast to east Africa, the Arabian peninsula, and Iran; and on the other, to southwest Asia and, through it, to southern China.

India has never been isolated, then. Only to the north do we find a steep barrier: the Himalaya mountain range. But in the northwest the range is broken by easily

This anonymous photograph shows the great durbar held in Delhi in 1903. The durbar was a sovereign's public assembly; under the Moghul dynasty it became a meeting of princes and dignitaries, called by the emperor. In this form it was passed down to the British viceroys, who heightened its ceremonial aspects with the aim of legitimizing the image of the British imperial mission. The durbar of 1903 was called for and organized by Lord Curzon in order to communicate to the princes the accession to the throne of Edward VII, the Queen Victoria's first-born. In the background we can see the Red Fort, built in the first half of the 17th century by the Moghul Emperor Shah Jahan; it became the heart of imperial government.

crossable gaps, such as the Khyber Pass, "gateway to India." Many peoples traveled over this pass, one after the other: the Indo-European Aryans, the Greeks of Alexander the Great, Arabs, Huns, Mongols, and Turks. Whether from an ethnic, religious, or cultural point of view, India appears as a sort of multicolored mosaic resulting from invasions, settlement, cultural encounters, and cross-cultural experiences. A variety of languages, ethnic groups, cultures, and religions has always set up obstacles to the country's unification. Even when two great imperial dynasties (the Maurya between the fourth and second century BC and the Gupta between the third and sixth century AD) extended their rule over much of the subcontinent, they never succeeded in covering it all. We could say that the first real form of national unity was created in India by the British.

On the northern edge of India, in the Karakorum and Himalayan ranges, we find the highest peaks in the world and many mountains that Hindus and Buddhists consider sacred. In the photo, the pyramid-shaped peak of Machhapuchhare.

A Brief Geography

In 1869, the year Gandhi was born, the population of the Indian subcontinent was about 250 million. Today, the same territory is home to approximately one and a quarter billion inhabitants — twenty percent of the entire world population — spread over 1.8 million square

miles. Of these 1,250 million, the majority (about 900 million) live in the State of India.

From north to south, from the snowy peaks of the Karakorum to the southernmost tip of the island of Sri Lanka, the Indian world stretches over 1800 miles and thirty degrees of latitude, from the thirty-seventh to the seventh parallel. This means that its northern tip lies at about the same latitude as Los Angeles, and its southern tip at the latitude of Yaoundé, the capital of Cameroon. The maximum width of the subcontinent, from the Indus delta to the delta of the Ganges, also approximates 1,800 miles. In the north we find a great arch making up the largest mountainous area in the world, and having at its center the soaring Karakorum and Himalaya ranges. At their feet lie an enormous low alluvial plain, called the Indo-Gangetic plain: that, too, is in the form of an arch.

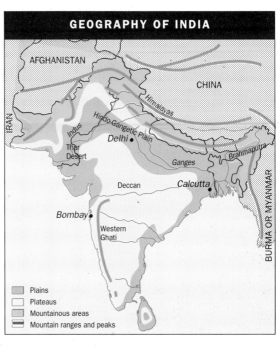

The rivers that engendered it and that drain it pour into the sea at two great deltas. Further southward, we find a peninsula shaped like an isosceles triangle, the Deccan: a vast highland of ancient lands, closed in on two sides by raised ridges (*ghati*, or steps).

The great rivers carrying melting snow and Himalayan glacial water southwards, together with the monsoon rains, keep India free of the bands of desert that stretch almost uninterruptedly one after the other along the Tropic of Cancer, from the Sahara to the Arabian peninsula, all the way to the southern regions of Iran and to Afghanistan. There is only one small desert, the Thar, in the northwest part of the subcontinent; a little further east, the plains are fertile, covered with crops and luxuriant forests.

Indian winters are mild, because the great northern ranges protect the subcontinent from the cold northern winds. Good weather predominates in January and February; rainfall is scarce or, in some areas, even nonexistent. In January, much of the subcontinent is as hot as midsummer Miami. In those months India is vibrant with people on the move, travelers of all sorts: from pilgrims journeying to sacred sites, to street peddlers trekking the roads from village to village.

From March to May the temperature rises daily, until it reaches an average of 95°F in some regions of the interior. Toward the end of this period, the heat becomes torrid and the atmosphere oppressive. Sudden flashes of lightning cut through a murky sky, accompanied by explosive rumbles of thunder. One waits anxiously for a storm that always seems about to burst, but then is late in coming. Insects invade people's dwellings. Many activities come to a halt; schoolchildren go on vacation. In some areas, food reserves often run out; some people are reduced to drinking water from murky pools. Cows and other emaciated animals wander about desperately, exhausted almost to the point of death, seeking relief from hunger

Lord and Lady Curzon during a tiger hunt in 1902. Lord Curzon was Viceroy of India (except for an interval of a few months) from 1899 to 1905.

and thirst. Seen from the air, much of India looks like a desert. The land is arid after the long drought, almost devoid of vegetation, and cut by deep cracks.

Finally, during June and July, the monsoon blows in. Heavy with humidity, it first appears off the west coast of the peninsula, then off the east coast, and finally, over Bengal. Its advent is highly violent and spectacular: it comes in the form of typhoons that swell the rivers till they overflow, tearing off the roofs of houses and huts. But finally people are able to sow, plants spring up, nature revives. A new season has begun: that of the great rains. It will last until September or October.

"Monsoon" is an Arab word meaning "season." In reality, the alternation between the dry winter monsoon (which blows from the interior of the continent) and the humid summer one, represents the only authentic climatic variation on the Indian subcontinent. Practically speaking, the seasons are two: a dry one and a wet one. Rainfall is heaviest along the west coast of the peninsula, in Sri Lanka, and in the northeast. In contrast, it rains very little in the Deccan interior, and even less in the Indus valley.

The most dramatic aspect of the Indian climate is the extreme variability of rainfall, its unpredictability. One year a monsoon may bring a great deal of rain, and the next, very little. Farmers can never tell ahead of time, and so are at the mercy of the rain's whims. Floods and periods of drought are the two great plagues. Though opposed to one another, they are both disastrous. They have always threatened the inhabitants of the region, in spite of the Indians' ancient skill in building dams and levees, intricate networks of canals, catchment basins and rainwater reservoirs.

The southwest and northeast, where the rivers and the

In northwest India we find the most arid zones of the subcontinent, including a true desert, the Thar, today shared by Pakistan and the Indian state of Rajasthan. In the photo, a camel caravan in search of water and pastures in more hospitable lands.
© Publifoto

The Ganges springs from a Himalayan glacier and flows southeast for 1,600 miles, parallel to the great range. After mixing its waters with those of the Brahmaputra, the two form a giant delta, which coincides with the historical region of Bengal (today divided between Bangladesh and the Indian state of West Bengal).

summer monsoons provide the greatest amounts of water, are kingdoms of wet tropical forest: the dense, luxuriant "jungle" of adventure novels. Until not long ago, elephants, tigers, and poisonous snakes used to roam there among trees as tall as 200 feet, beneath which stretched a thick, impenetrable layer of underbrush; today, farm crops have taken over much of the land, so that wild areas have shrunk. The Deccan is dominated by a humid savanna, covered with high grasses alternating with forests. The most arid zones of the peninsula are characterized by steppes and arid brush, as is much of the northwest. Finally, a conifer forest stretches up the Himalayan slopes as far as the line of permanent snows; because of the latitude, the tree line is quite high up.

This general picture has, however, been profoundly modified by man. In the northwest, where the climate would never tend to favor anything but an arid steppe, we find richly cultivated fields, thanks to fertile alluvial

soil and the farmers' skill. In the savanna areas, grass fails to grow tall, although it could potentially do so thanks to abundant rainfall: its growth is curtailed, at least in part, by animals searching for pastures. These creatures are particularly numerous in India. At any rate, it is the forests that have been most dramatically influenced by man's activity. The use of wood for fuel and construction, of vegetation for animal fodder, and above all, the need for arable land to provide food crops for a numerous and growing population have combined to shrink the forests substantially.

The Ganges is the most sacred river of India, a country where nearly every river is sacred. Myths say it descended from heaven to give relief to the thirsty land. Its entire course is marked by sanctuaries and other places of worship, and bathing in its waters washes away all sins. More prosaically, the Ganges offers water for irrigation, laundry, and every other need of the many villagers living along its banks.

A Glance at History: Origins to the Moghuls

Like early European texts — The *Histories of Herodotus*, for example — ancient Indian writing can be frustrating for the modern student of history. Their ancient writings, their classics (the *Vedas*, the *Upanishads*, and the two epic poems, the *Mahabharata* and the *Ramayana*), contain no dates, and generally we do not even know when or by whom they were written. They speak of kings and kingdoms, without telling us when those kings lived or when they flourished. Therefore, very few dates exist in India's ancient history.

The first inhabitants of India probably belonged to a group of dark-skinned peoples, the Dravids, who were later driven into the south of the peninsula, where their descendants live on. At least 200 million Indians, still, speak Dravidic languages, such as Telegu and Tamil. It was probably the Dravids who created the most ancient known Indian civilization, discovered thanks to the archaeological excavations that in this century uncovered the ruins of two cities, Mohenjo-Daro and Harappa. They lay along the course of the Indus. Built most probably in the third millenium BC, they were large cities, having streets up to thirty feet in width, and an elaborate drainage system.

Beginning around 1600 BC, India was invaded by successive waves of Aryan tribes. These Aryans spoke an Indo-European language; lighter-skinned than the Dravids, they came from the steppes of southern Russia. An ancient, learned language spoken by the Aryans, Sanskrit, is ancestor to the languages spoken by most of today's Indians: Hindi, Bihari, Bengali, etc.

The Aryan invaders were familiar with the wheeled cart, the horse, and metal-headed arrows. Some scholars believe that they destroyed and sacked the Dravids' cities, imposing their rule and forcing some of the darker-skinned people to flee southwards. Others believe that the Aryans, initially a nomadic people, became sedentary little by little, settling on the Indo-Gangetic plains and giving origin to a number of states. In reality, we cannot be certain that things really proceeded in this way. For example, we are sure that the Aryans not only raised cattle, but also were acquainted with agriculture, before arriving in India. Moreover, it seems quite probable that the destruction of the cities of Harappa and Mohenjo-Daro, during the first half

This sculpture of the 3rd-4th century AD, discovered at Hadda, Afghanistan, is preserved in the Guimet Museum in Paris. It is known as the "Genius of the Flowers," and — with many other works — bears witness to the fortuitous synthesis of Indian–Buddhist and Roman-Hellenistic art that characterized a part of present-day Afghanistan known as Gandhara.

of the second millenium BC, did not happen for military reasons (i.e., Aryan attack), but because of fire, natural catastrophes, or changes in climate. Finally, it is probable that processes of cultural exchange and fusion gradually occurred between the Aryans and Dravids, and that therefore, their relations were not necessarily (or at least, not always) of a violent nature.

In the fourth century BC, Alexander the Great invaded northwest India, crossing the Indus river and defeating a series of local princes. The excessive length of his lines of communication forced him to interrupt his expedition and turn back, but for several centuries, there existed in that part of India states governed by Greeks, and having close links to Greek culture.

We know that many other peoples later invaded India, usually by crossing over the mountain passes of the northwest. So it was for the Huns in the fifth and sixth century AD, the Arabs in the eighth, and for numerous Turkish-Mongolian peoples in the centuries that followed. In some instances, these peoples limited themselves to carrying out raids, superior though they were in military strength, and then making rapid retreats. At other times, they settled temporarily in the northwest regions: those which most reminded them of the environment they had left behind — the deserts and steppes of the Middle East and Central Asia. The invaders often stopped there, in that anteroom of India proper, without pushing into the

The great mausoleums of two sovereigns, both Muslim, who for a long period fought over possession of northern India in the 16th century. The first of these rises in Sasaram, in Bihar: it contains the remains of Sher Shah Suri, founder of a dynasty of Afghan origin who for some years (he reigned from 1533 to 1545) successfully opposed the Moghuls, newcomers to India.

The second is at Delhi, the "garden-tomb" of Humayun, second emperor of the Moghul dynasty, who reigned from 1530–1556. Both monuments show a synthesis of Islamic and Indian architectural elements.

strange, unknown environment of the tropical forest. But meanwhile, their continued contact with peoples who had embraced Islam ended up spreading this religion in India, too, especially in the north. During the same period, the Arabs were setting up an intricate commercial network on the Indian Ocean, touching the east coast of Africa, the Arab peninsula, and Malabar, the west coast of the Deccan.

At the beginning of the sixteenth century a new, Persian-speaking dynasty of Turkish-Mongolian extraction came on the scene. This population came from Afghanistan, and believed they were the descendants of Genghis Khan and Tamerlane. Little by little, they defeated one Indian kingdom after another, until they had succeeded in imposing their rule over vast areas of the subcontinent. Thus began the Moghul empire, destined to remain alive and well for three centuries.

While the penetration into India of other peoples — especially Muslims — was of a religious and commercial nature, often founded on force of arms, Indian expansion eastward revealed different characteristics. Penetration eastward pointed toward China and Mongolia in the northeast, and even more predominantly, toward Southeast Asia, and it proceeded peacefully, relying mostly on the fascination exercised by Indian culture and on journeys made by pilgrims and merchants. Buddhism, born in India in the sixth century BC, spread through China in the third century AD, and from there passed into Burma (today Myanmar), Thailand, and Indochina, which increasingly assumed the ideas and customs of Indian culture.

Arrival of the Europeans

The Europeans arrived at the end of the fifteenth century, led by the Por-

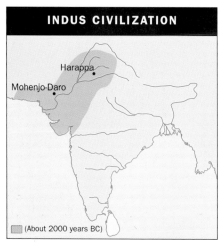

INDUS CIVILIZATION

Harappa

Mohenjo-Daro

(About 2000 years BC)

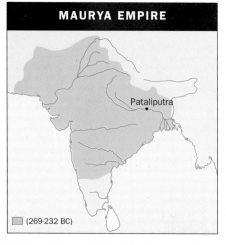

MAURYA EMPIRE

Pataliputra

(269-232 BC)

tuguese, Vasco da Gama. They landed at Calicut, a port on the Malabar coast, and discovered to their surprise that it was a center of international commerce, where one could find Jewish, Armenian, and North African Arab merchants.

From then on, and for nearly a century, the Portuguese adventurers sought for and found their fortune on these seas, unscrupulously eliminating their competitors. During the first twenty-five years of their presence in the region, they rigged out a total of 247 ships, which set off in flotillas for India nearly every year: a truly exceptional enterprise for a nation as poor and scarcely populated as Portugal. Subjected to this pressure from the Portuguese, the complex trade network which centuries of activity had woven among myriads of ports and peoples across Asia fell into a crisis. The fact that the Portuguese had arrived in India during a period when the subcontinent was tormented by dynastic rivalries and religious wars made it easier for them to conquer several important coastal cities.

However, the Portuguese were too weak to maintain control over the vast territories which they won in Asia: soon other European powers arrived, rivals among themselves. Between the seventeenth and eighteenth centuries, little by little, the Portuguese in India were shoved aside by the Dutch and the English, who had each organized great East Indies Companies. Later on, the Dutch would prefer to head eastward, to Indonesia. The English, on the contrary, opened trading agencies in Madras, Bombay, and Calcutta; and for a long time they were dedicated essentially to mercantile activities. Then, during the eighteenth century, they allowed themselves to become embroiled in the rivalries between different Indian states. Moreover, they found themselves forced

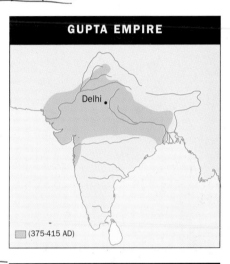

GUPTA EMPIRE

Delhi

(375-415 AD)

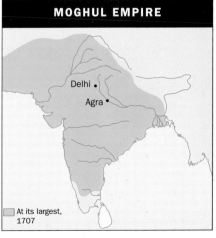

MOGHUL EMPIRE

Delhi

Agra

At its largest, 1707

to fight the imperial ambitions of the French, who had arrived in the meantime. Having begun almost by chance, the conquest of India by the British then continued without pause. Between 1757 (the year of Clive's victory over the Bengal sovereign) and the first half of the nineteenth century, the British took over India piece by piece, gradually subjugating the single states.

The British Conquest

Britain's conquest of India between the mid-eighteenth century and the first decades of the nineteenth, still represents for historians an unsolved problem, at least in part. The great European colonial conquests belong to the sixteenth and seventeenth century, though colonialism made a further lurch forward at the end of the last century, with the breaking up of Africa and the French occupation of Indochina. But in the seventy-year period starting in 1760

Robert Clive (1725–1774), a military man and administrator in the service of East India Company, was the first great "builder" of the British Empire in India. He was appointed Baron of Plassey, after the locality north of Calcutta where he had won a decisive battle in 1757. Later he fell into disgrace. This 1775 painting by Edward Penny, pictures him in the act of receiving from the son of the nabob of Bengal a sum for the aid of invalid soldiers and officers, and for the widows of soldiers killed in combat. India Office, London.

(the year when British India was born), the European colonial presence elsewhere in the world was forced to retreat on nearly every front: the British, the French, the Spanish, and the Portuguese lost their American colonies. The only exceptions during this period were the Russian advance into the Caucasus, the Dutch occupation of Indonesia, and as we have seen, the British conquest of India.

The relationship between the British conquest and the beginnings of the industrial revolution in India is more clearly understood by scholars. The protagonist of British expansion in Asia, that is, the East India Company, had been founded in 1600 by a group of merchants who had obtained from Queen Elizabeth a monopoly in trade with the Orient. In quite a traditional way, it represented a mercantile policy very different from the economic liberalism that provided an ideology for the industrial revolution. Moreover, for a long time the industrial revolution relied above all on the expansion of the textile industry in Lancashire, just when the Company, for its part, was importing textiles into Great Britain. (This it continued to do for a long period.) Later, as we shall see, the economic interests of this same Company and of many private dealers would be modified, and they would assume a more relevant role in the management of the conquered territories. But in the beginning, at least, it would be difficult to attribute to the Company an exclusive role as prime mover in Britain's conquest of a vast Indian empire.

At any rate, in the thought and writings of British officers, politicians, and entrepreneurs, we can find no coherent imperial plan — at least not until the early nineteenth century. On the contrary, such men tended to perceive and emphasize the risks of any possible conquests. Sir Thomas Roe, who had been the first ambassador of the British court to the Moghul empire between 1615 and 1619, had warned that one particular "rule" should be kept: profit should be sought on the seas and in peaceful trade; it was an error to maintain military posts and to fight battles on the Indian mainland.

Exactly a century and a half later, he was echoed by Robert Clive (who would nevertheless become one of the great "empire builders"): if the idea of conquest were to become the rule in British policy, Clive foresaw that Britain would inevitably be forced to go on acquiring territories, one by one, until the whole empire rebelled against it. And when that happened, Britain could hardly hope to find allies in its defense; and the Indians, left to their own devices, with no help from European allies, would find in their own strength the reason to wage an ever more "militant" war against the British occupiers.

*W*arren Hastings (1732–1818), the first governor of British India, from 1774–1785. Hastings and Robert Clive were the two great conquerors of India in the 18th century. A controversial figure, after his return to the homeland he was accused of corruption, but he was absolved after a long trial. The same thing had happened to Clive a few years before; after a verdict of innocence, he killed himself. This Indian watercolor, done around 1782, is preserved in the British Library.

As paradoxical as it may seem, then, the British would have preferred to go restrict their activities to the expansion of trade; when they dedicated themselves to conquest, they did so rather unwillingly, dragged into the struggles between different states and power groups in an era of disintegration, an era dominated by the crisis of the Moghul empire. It is within this Indian context that one must view the growing involvement of the British in local conflicts, which ended up in the progressive extension of their rule. Thus it was possible to witness the strange phenomenon of a small group of individuals gradually conquering a much larger and more populated empire than their own homeland: a phenomenon that astonished people at the time, and has created problems for historians ever since. Indeed, around 1770 the British subjects residing in India included only a few hundred officers of the East India Company, plus a few thousand soldiers. Furthermore, contrary to what is usually thought, the British did not at first enjoy technological military superiority but, at most, only naval superiority. Many local sovereigns acquired modern weapons from abroad and made use of European advisors in various capacities.

The conflict between the French and the British helped lead to the European conquest of the subcontinent. This painting by Francis Hayman shows the French surrender at Pondicherry in 1761 to the English colonel, Sir Eyre Coote. Two years later, with the treaty of Paris, this eastern coastal city would return to the French, who had possessed it since 1674. They kept it until 1954, eight years after Indian independence. National Army Museum, London.

However, after only a few decades the British succeeded in constructing a highly efficient military machine, which relied on two strong points. The first was discipline, organizational capacity, and moral solidity: qualities that were often lacking in Indian armies, and which turned out to be more important than military techniques. The second originated in the use of a great number of Indian soldiers (*sepoys*), attracted by good pay, recruited specifically from populations and castes of military tradition, or believed to be such (Sikhs, Pathans, Gurkhas, Rajputs). Their presence gave rise to the British theory of "warrior races." Even during the second half of the nineteenth century, when the British army grew to over 150,000 men, the British represented no more than a third of these (though nearly all the officers were British). It was therefore a predominantly Indian army that conquered India on behalf of Britain.

We should also remember that India did not have a tradition of unity, much less a sense of national community. At most, it had a series of loyalties to regional roots: but in many cases, these, too, were limited by cultural and ethnic diversity. In addition, throughout its history nearly all the subcontinent had known invasions and plundering, peaceful settlement and violent con-

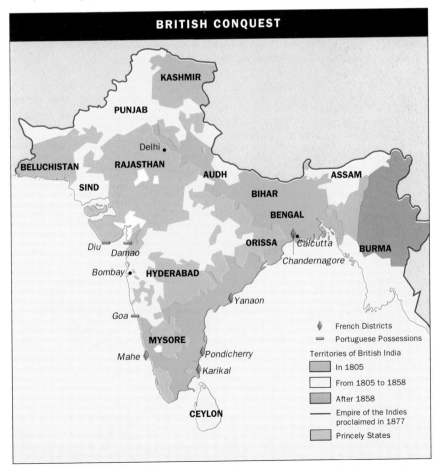

BRITISH CONQUEST

KASHMIR

PUNJAB

Delhi

BELUCHISTAN   RAJASTHAN

SIND   AUDH   ASSAM

BIHAR

BENGAL

Diu   ORISSA   Calcutta   BURMA

Damao   Chandernagore

Bombay   HYDERABAD

Yanaon

Goa

MYSORE   Pondicherry

Mahe   Karikal

CEYLON

♦ French Districts
= Portuguese Possessions
Territories of British India
In 1805
From 1805 to 1858
After 1858
— Empire of the Indies proclaimed in 1877
Princely States

quest. Even the last great empire, the Moghul, was of foreign origin — Turkish-Mongolian — and Muslim religion. In some cases the local dynasties had taken up arms against newcomers; in others they had accepted them quite peacefully.

In the eyes of most eighteenth-century Indians, the British did not appear to be "colonizers" (as they would later), but rather newcomers in a long series of immigrant groups. Some social groups, such as merchants and bankers, favored the new economic possibilities opened up by their presence. Some sovereigns thought they might turn the English into allies against their enemies, especially against the Moghuls; others feared them, for the opposite reason. Therefore, to view the British in India in the second half of the eighteenth century as colonizers and conquerors, is only possible in hindsight. It is more correct to say that for a few decades, they acted as a fulcrum of political power in India.

Another element favoring the British was their careful accommodation of the institutions, laws, and customs of the Indians. The other great empire builder, alongside Clive, was Warren Hastings. In 1784 he wrote that until only a short time before, the inhabitants of India had been considered by many Europeans as little more than savages; this prejudice, noted Hastings, had not yet been totally uprooted, though it had been weakened. Any chance to observe the Indians' true character, he wrote, should lead to a more generous preoccupation with their natural rights, which should be considered on the same plane as those of Europeans. Indian literature, rich with examples of humanity, would survive long after the cessation of British rule.

Hastings was not simply an open-minded administrator and man of action; he was also an enthusiastic scholar and a sincere admirer of Indian culture. Not only did he have the Company set aside funds for the development of education, but in 1784 he also supported the foundation of the Asiatic Society of Calcutta, preparing the groundwork for Oriental studies. The fame of Eastern philosophies thus began to flourish in Europe; soon, Schopenhauer would point to India as the homeland of wisdom and tolerance; and the French philosopher,

This photograph from about 1900 shows one of the most picturesque points on the left bank of the Ganges, at Benares (Varanasi). In this city, sacred to the Hindus and dedicated to Shiva, temples, inns for pilgrims, and the houses of maharajas rise up along the river bank. Crowds of pilgrims make purifying ablutions here in the holy river. The right bank of the river, though, is considered unlucky; no Hindu would dare bathe there.

Victor Cousin, would call it the supreme "birthplace of philosophy," in contrast, he opined, to the poor results reached by "European genius."

The situation gradually changed as Britain increasingly took over the Company, limiting its powers to control the burgeoning empire. Although we cannot speak of a full-fledged form of racism until the second half of the century, the early 1800s saw a growth of the conviction that European and British culture were decidedly superior to Indian culture which was increasingly thought to be corrupt, immoral, cruel, and superstitious. Eventually the British came to believe it was their duty to uproot it for the sake of the higher interests of civilization and even for the Indians themselves. Whereas the early conquerors and merchants of the Company had developed a certain respect for Indian culture, to the point of opposing the entrance of Christian missionaries into the country (who would have risked upsetting the good relationship they held with the Indians), the new administrators assumed a profoundly different attitude. If we bear in mind Hastings's reference to the perennial values of Indian literature, we can clearly perceive the change of attitude reflected in a report written by T. B. Macaulay in the early 1830s. He wrote that a single shelf of English books was worth more than all the literature of India and Arabia, and that all the historical information written in Sanskrit is worth less than the history in the most mediocre English middle school manual. What is more, Macaulay maintained that one should substitute traditional Indian education with British education, in order not to continue teaching at public expense a medicine unworthy of an English blacksmith, an astronomy that would make an English schoolgirl laugh, a history packed full of twenty-foot tall kings and 3,000 year old kingdoms, and a geography based on seas of syrup and butter.

Macaulay combined this scorn for Indian cultures with an extraordinarily idealistic trust in the power of renewal and transformation that the introduction of British culture would have over the Indian people. In 1833, he wrote that the public conscience in India might develop so well under the British system as to overcome the system itself; that by way of good government, the British might teach their subjects to govern themselves even better; and that once educated in the ways of Western wisdom,

they might request institutions similar to British ones. Macaulay admitted he did not know when the day would come; but he would never attempt to prevent it or delay it. That day would be the most glorious one in British history.

Actually, something similar would occur, though very differently than the English politician and historian had predicted. Some Indian intellectuals would be "Westernized" in British schools, and would then claim rights and demand freedom and autonomy. In contrast others would see the imposition of a foreign culture as an outrage, and would thus be driven to start a rebirth of Hinduism, and to make even more radical demands for liberty and independence.

India under the Raj

In the middle of the nineteenth century, the British conquest of India had been nearly completed, and the immense colony seemed headed for pacification. But 1857 saw the revolt of the sepoys, the Indian mercenaries of the East India Company.

The Indian Mutiny, as it came to be called, was long and bloody, and it took the British a long time to repress it. This revolt has been seen both as the last tremor of resistance from the old "feudal" India and as the "first war of Indian independence." At any rate, it bore witness to the fact that opposition to the conquest had

Parade for a durbar of the Moghul Emperor Akbar II (1806–1837). On one of the elephants we see the "British resident" with his collaborators. After the second half of the 18th century, the Moghul emperor exercised rule which was little more than nominal and symbolic, under British control. The last emperor of the dynasty would be dismissed and exiled in 1858. India Office, London.

*H*anging of rebels during the sepoy revolt, or Indian Mutiny, of 1857–1858. The photograph was taken by Felice A. Beato, a Venetian who had been naturalized as British; he was one of the first, most adventurous and crudely realistic war reporters during the last century. After documenting some particularly violent, cruel moments of the revolt (and its repression), Beato went to China to witness the second Opium War. He then published a book of photographs on the landscapes and customs of Japan; went back to photograph more massacres in China; and was present in Sudan, at the retaking of Khartoum. Besides being a forerunner of modern sensational reportage, he was also considered a master of technique: he used mostly silver plates and albumin prints.

never been wholly snuffed out, particularly in states such as Bengal or Maharashtra, which had first strenuously opposed the Moghul invaders, and then the British.

The revolt was quelled with a great deal of toil and bloodshed; then the British government took away the Company's power to rule, claiming that for itself in the person of a viceroy. Public servants replaced the Company functionaries. By now, the entire subcontinent lay in the hands of the British, although they allowed approximately 500 princely states to survive (the states governed by maharajas), whose sovereignty was little more than a formality. Finally, in 1877, Queen Victoria was solemnly proclaimed "Empress of India:" India was now the most splendid jewel of the crown, and the British Raj ("dominion") had reached its apex. In order to protect the boundaries of their Indian empire, the British also took possession of nearby territories in Afghanistan and Burma.

The Mutiny of 1857 had important effects on Anglo-Indian relations, too. The British came out nominally victorious, but wounded and worried about the future. The "residents" herded together, closing themselves into their own settlements and their exclusive clubs. Their relations with the Indians were practically reduced to administrative duties and gestures of courtesy in the courts of the maharajas; or to treatment as subordinates (shoals of domestic servants quietly inhabited British houses). The respect which had characterized earlier times was replaced by an arrogance, founded on the deep conviction of their cultural superiority. This post-Mutiny India is pitilessly described by E.M. Forster in *A Passage to India*, and by George Orwell in *Burmese Days*.

British rule in India lasted in varying forms for about two centuries, and left deep scars in the country. Under British rule, for the first time the immense territory of the subcontinent was unified under a single government. In order to get around the obstacle of India's incredible variety of languages, the rulers imposed the use of their own; and even today, in India and Pakistan, many of the main newspapers are written in English, just as schools and universities continue faithfully to reproduce the educational and scholastic systems imported from England. The British supervised the building of a railway which is still the fourth largest in the world, but it was designed above all to favor their commercial and military interests. In fact, as the Mutiny itself made evident, they needed rapid means to move not only their merchandise, but also their troops, when revolts broke out. While it is true that the British introduced a number of modern innovations, we must also remember that in India, they pursued above all their own interests as the most far-reaching imperial power in the world. This led them to exploit India's resources, and, in the opinion of many, delay India's economic development. India sadly shared this fate with all the countries of Asia and Africa that were victims to European colonialism.

A *Gatling machine gun used by the British army during the battle of Kandahar, which ended the second Afghan war (1878–1880). On that occasion the British intervened beyond the Khyber Pass, interfering with Afghan dynastic matters in order to prevent Russia's expansion in the region.*

The most ancient religion of India is documented in the first great sacred books, the Vedas, and in epic poems like the *Mahabharata* and the *Ramayana*, written in Sanskrit (the forebear of India's modern Indo-European languages). The concept of the transmigration of souls after death into another living being soon appeared in Indian culture, and was thereafter to remain central to Indian religious thought. Eventually, the Vedic religion took on an increasingly ritualistic character, founded on the sacrifices offered by priests ("Brahmins") to the gods, on behalf of the community.

It was the reaction to this ritualism that drove the great religious reformers of the sixth and fifth centuries BC. The most famous of these is Gautama Siddharta, known as the Buddha (the "illuminated one"). While meditating over the pain and unhappiness of human existence, Siddharta discovered that these are engendered by the desire for riches, power, success, honor. Renouncing desire for these things, giving up the temptations of the world, leads to a perfect serenity of spirit, Nirvana. Nirvana will free one from the painful cycle of transmigration. **Buddhism** spread a sweet, serene morality of universal love, purity, non-violence, and detachment from worldly things. A man of Buddha's time, Mahavira, also called Jina, was the founder of **Jainism**. It, too, preached asceticism and absolute non-violence: even to-

day, Jainist monks sweep the path in front of them as they walk, so as not to risk killing some small animal. We can, however, say that the two religions, even while leaving a deep mark on Indian culture and religiosity, eventually suffered defeat. Jainism is practiced today by fewer than three million people, and Buddhism, by 4.7 million (while its followers in other parts of the world number about 300 million). In India, Buddhism threatened the power of the priests, the Brahmins, since it taught that man can be liberated without intermediaries, through his re-

lationship with the Absolute. The Brahmins reacted against this doctrine, and they won, but not without submitting their rivals to torture and persecution; though perhaps the defeat of Buddhism was also due to its advocating detachment from the world and flight from society. In contrast, Hinduism never attempted to flee from existing society, but rather accepted it, justified it, and impregnated it with itself. Practiced in India by about 600 million people (eighty percent of the population), today **Hinduism** is the most widespread religion. **Islam** is second, with more than ninety million followers. The Muslims remaining in India after the 1947 partition and the birth of Pakistan are so numerous that they make India one of the four countries in the world with the most Muslims (after Indonesia, and nearly equal with Pakistan and Bangladesh).

Christians number about sixteen million, and are mostly Catholics. The Punjab Sikhs — about twelve million — plus the six million living in other states of the union, are monotheistic.

Like the Buddhists and Jains, they reject castes. They never cut their beards or hair, which they wear caught up on top of their heads, in a sort of knotted scarf when children, and in a turban when adults.

Finally, the **Parsi** of Bombay, Mazdeists (or Zoroastrians), are the descendants of Persians who emigrated in ancient times in order to flee the religious persecution perpetrated by Muslims. Both Sikhs and Parsis are active, enterprising minorities. The Parsi, whose male followers all dress in Western style, have always been leaders in cultural and economic life: for example, the powerful Tata family of entrepreneurs are Parsi, as is the famous orchestra conductor, Zubin Mehta. Today, however, they are in a serious phase of demographic decline: there were 100,000 in 1961, while now there are only 58,000. This decline is due to the growing difficulty of marriage (Parsis marry only among themselves), and to the strong tendency to emigrate to the United States, Canada, and Australia.

It is not easy to define Hinduism. First of all, it is not a church, in the sense that we attribute to that word, but rather a complex and variegated mass of rites and mythologies, Vedic elements and suc-

cessive philosophies, and local cults. There exists a learned Hinduism inspired by philosophy and mysticism, and a popular one, formed

mainly by social ritual and customs. Buddhism has also left a mark on the older religion, in its respect for the sanyasi, "he who renounces," the man who chooses the path of poverty, spiritual perfection, and abandonment of worldly joys for the sake of a deeper truth.

The Hindu pantheon is densely populated, but dominated by a triad, the "sacred Trimurti": Brahma, the creator; Shiva, the destroyer, lord of death; and Vishnu, the benevolent protector of Life. However, these divinities appear in a number of avatara or incarnations: for example, Krishna and Rama (the god most beloved by Gandhi) are incarnations of Vishnu. In addition, each individual Indian can choose the divinity he prefers, in order to worship it and ask it for protection. One of the most loved and popular gods is Ganesha or Ganapati, "he who sweeps away obstacles" — the protector of travelers, but also of thieves and scholars. Many goddesses are de-

voutly worshipped too; they are usually companions to one of the major gods: for example, Lakshmi, companion to Vishnu, or the fearsome, many-armed Durga, Shiva's wife. The customs and forms of worship are varied, too. A sacred dimension accompanies every moment of daily life, which is regulated by prayers, rites, superstitions, and talismans. People make pilgrimages for thousands of miles in order to pray in particularly venerated places or to purify themselves in the waters of the Ganges, especially at the holy city of Benares (Varanasi). ∎

On previous page, the statue of the Buddha Maitreya. From Gandhara, it dates back to the 4th century BC. Musée Guimet, Paris.
Left, a popular image depicting the god Ganesh.
Above, the Golden Temple at Amritsar, a Sikh sanctuary.
© Publifoto.

A group of cotton carders in a photo taken by William Johnson, just after the mid-nineteenth century. India Office, London.

When the British began their conquest of India, the region's economy lagged behind those of the European countries of the time. However, it possessed a number of small crafts industries, particularly for the production of cotton textiles. Though the Indians used antiquated tools, they were able to weave high-quality cloth. But little by little, the British began to export raw cotton to England, finding it cheaper to process it in the more modern British factories, and re-export it as fabric. The outcome was that Indian handicrafts fell into decline, finding it impossible to meet the competition from British industry.

By using modern machinery, the British managed to furnish products at a much cheaper price, though at times they were of inferior quality. It was British industry that profited from this relationship between the colony and the colonial powers. In fact, the Indian economy was so heavily damaged by British competition that it fell into stagnation, or even declined. According to some scholars, economic backwardness was thus a price paid by

India in order to contribute to the transformation of Great Britain into the richest and most advanced European country.

Indian agriculture was profoundly transformed by British rule, too. Before the British Raj, India was, in fact, a giant grouping of tiny villages, each of which was self-sufficient, though poverty was the norm. Each village, that is, produced the essential goods that its inhabitants needed: from cereals to vegetables, from fruit to milk. Even clothes and work tools — hoes, for example — were made within the village, by an artisan or by the peasants themselves, who dedicated themselves to handicrafts when they had free time off from the fields.

Only for a few goods (such as salt) was it necessary to rely on the work of merchants living outside the village. Except for such cases, practically no relations existed between one village and another, or between village and state. The only connection with state government existed in the person of an officer in charge of collecting yearly taxes from the peasants; each village, that is, paid out a given percentage of its crops. Of course there were the exploiters and there were the exploited, in Indian villages. Some families were privileged, and others were poor (mostly those belonging to the lower castes). But there were also forms of solidarity, and mutual assistance, which made it easier for the peasants to face hard times, famine, or misfortune.

Vellore train station, in southern India, around 1880.

This ancient form of social organization, which had survived without change for centuries, was broken by colonial policy. In many regions, the British actually transformed the tax collector into the owner of the territory over which he had jurisdiction. Whereas formerly the land had been owned in common by the village, now a restricted group of owners came to possess larger and larger tracts of territory. They soon found it cheaper to produce goods for exportation, especially those which were in high demand in England, rather than the wheat or rice needed to feed the peasants.

India thus became blanketed by large plantations of cotton, jute, tea, and indigo, on which thousands of peasants, now devoid of land, worked as day laborers in frequently inhuman conditions. The big landowners thus prospered, as did the large British companies, while famine increasingly threatened the Indian peasants. Between 1850 and 1900 there were twenty-four periods of famine, which caused more than twenty million deaths.

Indian Intellectuals and European Culture

When European culture arrived in the nineteenth century, China and Japan responded with an attitude of resistance and closure. This did not occur in India, except as a marginal reaction of small minorities. Of course, it must be considered that the Europeans came to India accompanied by, or under the protection of, political domination; whereas both China and Japan preserved a form of national independence.

But this does not suffice to explain the phenomenon. India had always welcomed cultural influences from abroad, and so it was in the case of European culture. For many Indian intellectuals, the arrival of European culture represented both a challenge and a fine opportunity for renewal. Acceptance of a culture which appeared as a rational, efficient herald of modernity characterized several important figures who were highly influential during the nineteenth century. One of these was Henry L.V. Derozio (1809–1831), born in Calcutta of a family of Portuguese-Anglo-Indian descent. Derozio attended a school directed by a Scottish follower of the Enlightenment, and came out an advocate for the total westernization of India. He wrote verse in the style of Byron. He was a professor at the Hindu College, the first modern educational institution

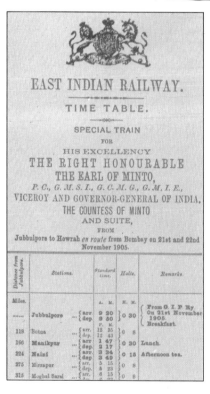

When a viceroy traveled with his retinue, luxurious trains were specially prepared for him. Special timetables were printed for the occasion, like this one for the journey of Lord Minto in 1905.

in India, created in Calcutta in 1816, and founded a society of free thinkers, as well as a newspaper, *The East Indian*. Nothing so strange about that: except that all these activities were performed in the space of twenty-two years, the few short years making up the life of this bright and unfortunate young man who was killed by cholera.

Ram Mohan Roy (1772–1833) lived longer and was destined to greater fame. A Brahmin officer of the East India Company, he was a man of great culture, especially well-versed in the field of languages and religions. His thought was influenced by Hindu, Muslim, and Christian ideas. The resulting product, however, was fundamentally European: indeed, Ram Mohan Roy was a late follower of Humanism and the Enlightenment.

In this 1815 engraving by Thomas Rowlandson, a Hindu woman immolates herself on her husband's funeral pyre. The practice of sati was prohibited by Lord Bentinck in 1829.

A deist, he agreed with the missionaries' criticism of superstition, idolatry, and polytheism; he viewed the castes as the priests' corruption of the original Hindu texts; he fought against the subjugation of women, as symbolized by the harem and by *purdah*, the separation between men and women in many areas of daily life. He wanted to abolish polygamy and *sati*, the custom of sacrificing the widow on her husband's funeral pyre that was widely practiced in the higher castes. These were the objectives of the Brahmo Samaj, the society founded by Roy, which intended to transform Hinduism into a religion comparable to Western religions, but refined by rationalism (thus challenging the missionary movement). He was succeeded in leadership of the Brahmo Samaj by Dwarkanath, then by Debendranath Tagore, respectively the grandfather and the father of the famous poet who would win the Nobel Prize in 1913. Similar societies fought in favor of marriage for widows, women's education, and the abolition of child marriage and castes.

From birth, every Hindu belongs to a caste. A caste is a social group presenting various characteristics:
1) endogamy, i.e., the obligation of marrying only within one's own caste;
2) exercise of the same occupation by all members;
3) observance of religious rites, customs' and dietary rules particular to the caste;
4) rigid hierarchical placement in relation to other social groups.

Castes are closed groups; it is impossible for an individual to pass into a higher caste. A person born into a given caste will die in it, unless his bad behavior causes his fall into the status of the "casteless": that is, a social group considered to be inferior to all the others.

The origin of castes is very ancient, and still widely debated by scholars. The word "caste" is of Portuguese origin; today it is used in India too, but Indians prefer to speak of *varna* ("color") in order to designate the four major groupings: first, the priests or Brahmins; then the warriors, or *kshatriya*; the *vaisya*, artisans and merchants; and the *sudra*, or peasants, poorer artisans, and servants. The casteless are the lowest on the social scale. These are the pariahs, the untouchables; Gandhi, who fought for their emancipation, called them *harijan*, "children of God." Today the casteless prefer to define themselves as *dalit*, the "oppressed," indicating that they wish not to be seen as objects of pity, but as active subjects claiming their rights.

Today, the *varna* structure can be considered a theoretical model, more than a concrete reality. Ancient Indian society may have known this four-section division (plus one: the outcast); but as time passed, each of the four *varna* has broken up into a multitude of subgroups, those we find in real-life India today under the name of *jati* (meaning "birth"). Each of the *jati* presents those same characteristics mentioned above: closure, endogamy, occupational specialty, hierarchical placement, and so on.

This breaking up of castes into minor groups came about through geographical, historical, ethnic, and linguistic causes. The current names for the *jati* refer mainly to occupations, but may also designate extraction, tribe, sect, or geographic site. They vary from one place to another.

The separation between one caste and another is virtually absolute. In a given village, each caste lives in its own neighborhood, avoiding all contact with inferior castes, and particularly with the untouchables. Even casual contact with a person of a lower caste is a stain that must be washed out by particular rites. No orthodox Brahmin would ever eat food cooked by a member of a low caste. Duties and rules of behavior are also very rigid. Each caste is characterized by its own level of "purity," which is both physical and moral. At the top of the hierarchy of values we find cleanliness and hygiene, but above all, culture and everything of a spiritual nature. At the bottom lie the elements of nature and organic life, from animal blood to human refuse.

The untouchables are the only ones who can exercise the despised "impure" occupations: hunter, fisherman, butcher, tanner, streetsweeper, grave digger. Food, too, has its levels of purity: eating vegetables is less impure that eating meat (the overwhelming majority of Brahmins are vegetarians); eating game is less impure than eating the meat of domestic animals who were nourished on garbage and raised by people of lower castes; eating the meat of herbivorous animals is less impure than eating the meat of carnivorous ones.

It is Hinduism, above all, which supports and nurtures the caste system, particularly through the doctrine of the transmigration of souls. A person who leads an honest life, in harmony with the cosmic order, respectful of the rules of his or her caste, can hope to pass into a superior caste in a future transmigration, until reaching that supreme level of purity allowing his or her dissolution into the Absolute, thus escaping the cycle of migrations, which Hinduism regards as a curse. (Of course, bad behavior can cause transmigration into a lower caste level, or into an animal.) The Hindu is animated by this hope of promotion after death. He or she does not consider inequality at birth as being unjust, but rather sees in it the

expression of universal order and justice. If one is born a sudra, it is because one's preceding lives have destined this to be so. Furthermore, one's caste provides solidarity and protection. Even among the untouchables, the great majority still believe that their miserable situation is due to divine will, and hope for a better future life. All these characteristics make the caste system the most perfect one possible for preserving a hierarchical society, since (unlike social classes as we know them) it is founded on the individual's total acceptance of his or her status. It is significant

that the struggle against caste divisions in contemporary India has been conducted with a great deal of prudence (and with very modest results), for fear of offending deeply-rooted religious beliefs. And it is also significant that the great majority of caste conflicts that we know of have as protagonists the casteless, the outcasts, the poorest of the poor. ■

Left, a Deccan 17th-century miniature depicts a Brahman intent on making a ritual offering. Above, three "untouchables" in a village near Madras, on the east coast of India.

The position of Swami Dayananda Sarasvati (1824–1883) was more complex. Influenced by the writings of European philologists and linguists, who discovered the Indo-European languages and re-discovered the great classics of ancient India, Dayananda interpreted the Veda as holy scriptures revealed by God, just as the Bible and the Qur'an were, and found in them a monotheistic message.

His attitude was two-sided. On one hand, he joined the campaign for modernization, both by accepting European schools and by combating the prohibition of widows marrying, the dietary taboos, forms of popular Hinduism stigmatized by Christian missionaries as superstitious, untouchability, membership in a caste from birth: all elements that he did not find in the *Veda*, and which he thus condemned as erroneous, later additions. On the other hand, unlike the more radical westernized Indians, he set himself up as a defender of Hinduism (though in a purified, renewed version), making it the pillar of Indian civilization, which he dreamed of restoring to the Vedic "golden age." His very choice of a name for the society which he founded in Bombay in 1875, Arya Samaj, which implies an acquaintance with studies concerning the Indo-European Aryans, contains a germ of that sectarianism which was later to antagonize other religious communities. In a sense, it prepared the way for nationalistic, extremist tendencies within Hinduism.

In our century, rightist nationalist parties such as Hindu Mahasabha ("Great Hindu Assembly") and Rashtriya Swayamsevak Sangh (RSS, "Association of National Volunteers") would take inspiration from Arya Samaj. Such parties are anti-Western, but also anti-Muslim, and advocate violent methods of struggle (particularly the RSS, which has a paramilitary organization at its disposal).

The nationalistic and religious reaction against westernization also received some impetus from Swami Vivekananda (Narendranath Datta, 1862–1902), who criticized the selfishness and materialism of European civilization. A Bengali, he received a Western education, but was also influenced by the mystic writer, preacher, and speaker, Ramakrishna. Vivekananda was perhaps the first great ambassador of "Indian wisdom" in the

Rudyard Kipling (1864–1938), portrait by Sir Philip Burne-Jones (1899). Rightly considered the official poet of the imperial mission of Great Britain, Kipling was born in Bombay, the son of a British government official, and lived for a long time in India, especially in Punjab, working as a journalist. His stories offer vivid images not only of the Anglo-Indian world, but more generally, of India during his time.

world, a forerunner of the Aurobindos and the Krishnamurtis. Within the Hindu tradition, Vivekananda opposed an exaggerated kind of contemplative life, while reassessing the value of ethics and engagement on this earth. He did not believe in a religion "that would not dry the eyes of a widow nor raise a piece of bread to the mouth of an orphan."

The Muslim world in India was also shaken by contact with European culture, and reacted by forming both modernizing groups and schools and fundamentalist ones. The former were exemplified by the current of thought which in 1906 would give rise to the Muslim League; in contrast, fundamentalism led to the Jamaat-i-Islami, born in 1941 through the initiative of Abul-Ala Maududi, and ideologically linked to its near contemporaries, the Egyptian Muslim Brotherhood.

Birth of a Nationalist Movement
The fact that India's resources were drained by its foreign rulers became increasingly clear to the starving peasants, to the failing artisans, and to those intellectuals who, though they had studied in British schools and earned diplomas, were rarely able to occupy posts of

Victoria Station in Bombay, in a painting by A.M. Haig (circa 1880). Like many other buildings of the colonial era, especially in Calcutta and Bombay, Victoria Station unites European architectural elements (Gothic, in this case) with others of the Indian tradition.

prestige in the administration, since it was nearly always the British who did so.

Paradoxically, though, the conditions of British rule actually helped the diverse Indian nationalist movement begin. During its long history, as we have seen, India had never been united; at the moment when the British arrived, in the midst of the crisis of the Moghul empire, political division had reached an extreme. This lack of unity had always prevented the development of a true Indian national consciousness. India had never vigorously opposed foreign invasion. Very often, it had viewed this as simply another normal change of dynasties.

So it was in the case of the British. If the British were not particularly loved, this was not so much because of their foreignness as their style of governing: for example, their imposition of British lifestyles, their hostility to traditional Indian customs, and their economic policy. We may therefore say that unification of

the country under one rule, that of the British viceroy, was a necessary step for the formation of an Indian national consciousness, and for its consolidation in the struggle for independence. Among other things, for the first time, unification allowed ideas to circulate and confront each other throughout the entire subcontinent.

A second helpful characteristic of British domination lay in the fact that Britain was a small country with the task of administrating, through the efforts of a fairly restricted number of men, an enormous territory. To do so, they sought out the collaboration of "educated," westernized Indians. In the nineteenth century the British were respected in Europe and the world for their liberal representative bodies. The fact that they were supposed to represent the vanguard of European liberalism made it very difficult for the British to found their dominion on repressive violence alone. Therefore, the British did not oppose the creation of schools or political and cultural

A typical British club around 1910. In these exclusive circles, where people held parties and played golf, polo, and cards, or simply read newspapers and chatted, the British residing in India attempted to recreate lifestyles similar to those they had left in their homeland.

societies, at least not when these did not challenge British sovereignty.

The Indian National Congress, which would later follow India's path toward independence, was originally not a true political party (it would become so many years later, thanks to Gandhi). It was, instead, a meeting of notables from every area of India, which took place each year in a different city. It gathered for the first time in 1885, under the auspices of the viceroy and with the participation of several Englishmen. Its president, W.C. Bonerjea, spoke of the "sentiments of national unity born during the reign of our beloved viceroy, Lord Ripon." Two British men, a Scottish merchant from Calcutta and an ex-functionary of the famous Anglo-Indian bureaucracy, presided over the Congresses of 1888 and 1889.

During its first years of life, the Congress represented a meeting place for the furtherance of interests which were no less British than they were Indian. On one hand, the British were interested in providing the burgeoning nationalist movement with a forum where activities and debates could take place under the more or less direct control of government authorities. Furthermore, they wished to speed up the formation of an Indian administrative class that would be willing to collaborate with the government in managing an empire too vast and complex for the numerically small forces of the British bureaucracy and the British military. The rulers' needs in such cases coincided with those of an upper middle class, an Indian elite made up of intellectuals, merchants, and entrepreneurs asking to perform a more active role in administration. This elite did not challenge British sovereignty in India, but asked the rulers to be consistent with the ideas that they professed in their homeland. As the motherland of modern freedoms, Great Britain could not help recognizing the justice of

Right, Lord Lytton, Viceroy of India between 1876 and 1880. The son of novelist E.G. Bulwer-Lytton, he too was the author of poems, under the pseudonym of Owen Meredith. This type of portrait laden with symbolism confirms the British rulers' taste for pomp and ceremony in the management of their imperial mission. It was during the viceroyship of Lytton that Queen Victoria (above, in a painting of 1863 by Sir George Hayter, in the National Gallery, London) was proclaimed Empress of India, during the first great British durbar (in Delhi, 1877).

equal rights for the Indian members of its empire. The British were criticized, then, for applying "non-British" principles in India by denying equal rights to the Indian populace. The most representative figures of Congress, such as Gopal Krishna Gokhale and Dadabhai Naoroji (just to name two men that Gandhi greatly admired and respected), intended to fight with constitutional methods for the introduction of representative bodies open to Indian membership. Another motivation for the struggle was opposition to the continual "draining off" of Indian wealth and resources (for example, by making Indians themselves pay taxes for the maintenance of the empire).

At any rate this Indian elite, formed in Anglo-Indian schools and often completing their studies in London, influenced by the Enlightenment and Utilitarianism, were more than willing to collaborate actively with the government in the diffusion of modern hygiene, and in the struggle against ancient prejudice and superstition.

For a long period of time, the exponents of political moderation held unrivalled sway over the Indian nationalist movement. But by the end of the century, many of the moderates' efforts had failed. The reduction of resource "drainage" was ridiculously low; and British reforms had granted almost no space for Indian participation in administering the country and making political decisions. Such failures were all the more discouraging because they were accompanied by the pressure of growing masses of educated young men who received no adequate social opportunities — either from civil institutions or economic structures. Such social phenomena coincided with a rebirth, in various forms, of Hinduism, and with a traditionalist reaction against modernization.

Toward the end of the nineteenth century, nationalism assumed a religious hue: indeed, it deliberately used religion to organize itself. Many Bengali writers re-evaluated the myths and historical facts of the Hindu tradition. In a novel written by one of them, Bankim Chandra Chatterji, a group of courageous patriots sings a hymn, *Bande Mataram*, which would later become the nationalists' hymn, and is India's national anthem today. *Bande Mataram* means "I honor the Mother," and the Mother, offended by foreign domination and awaiting salvation, is India herself, identified with the goddess Kali, a renewed and widely popular cult.

The figure who best revealed these new developments in Indian nationalism (or at least, that sector of it which has come to be known as "extremist") was Bal Gagandhar Tilak, a Mahratta Brahmin who lived from 1856 to 1920. Although he was also a Veda scholar, Tilak, unlike Dayananda or Vivekananda, was a politician, not a religious reformer; but as a politician, he centered much of his activity around religious themes. For example, he opposed a law raising the minimum age for marriage: not because he was against its actual principles, but because he denied that any foreign government had the right to interfere in the customs and traditions of the Indian people. For the same reason, when Bombay was struck by an outbreak of plague, he joined and led a mass protest against the brutality with which the soldiers had gone into homes to disinfect them.

Tilak utilized the defense and rebirth of Hinduism for nationalist ends: thus, for example, he turned the cult of the god Ganapati into a symbol of patroitism, and promoted annual celebrations in honor of Shivaji, who had headed the seventeenth century Mahratta resistance movement against the Moghuls. This political line led him to break with the Muslims.

An advocate of radical methods of political struggle, Tilak spent a total of seven years in prison, during two separate periods. This added to his prestige as leader of the "extremists." He came to be called the *Loka-*

Lokamanya Tilak, leader of the Indian "extremists" between the last years of the nineteenth century and 1920, the year of his death.

THE TEMPTATIONS OF TERRORISM

manya, "revered by the people," and was regarded as the main theorist and inspiring voice of Indian "extremism." Critical of the strategy of the moderates, ironically summed up as the formula of the "three p's" (pray, please, protest), he rejected the idea of Indian participation in the British power structure, favoring instead a complete *swaraj* ("self-government") as the final objective. He also pondered over the problem of winning over the masses to the anti-British struggle,

but here his caste identity hampered him; except in a few isolated cases, Tilak reached only rather restricted groups of intellectuals, students, and the politicized middle classes.

While it is true that Tilak's life acutely symbolized the new tendencies which solidified at the turn of the century, many other figures were moving along the same or similar paths; a number of movements and secret sects were forming in Punjab, Maharashtra, and Bengal. Mazzini, a fighter for Italian independence, became especially famous. His works were translated into several Indian languages, until his influence was replaced by that of the Russian nihilists.

An English lady (a memsahib) carried in a rickshaw somewhere in southern India, circa 1895.

In the nationalist propaganda of the early years of the century, the parallel between India and czarist Russia was widespread. Both were denounced as autocratic countries, characterized by the domination of an omnipotent, aggressive bureaucracy. In India as in Russia, terrorism was thus portrayed by many as being the only possible road to liberty.

Political pamphlets written on these themes appeared only a short time before the stashing of secret deposits of weapons, munitions, and bombs. Almost immediately, contacts sprang up between Russian terrorists and would-be Indian terrorists. In 1906, after the murder of several people in the villa of the Russian Prime Minister Stolypin, an influential Anglo-Indian news sheet of Allahabad, *The Pioneer*, while condemning the "horror of such crimes" also recognized that terrorism was the only method of political struggle left to a populace at war with "despotic rulers." Having dissolved the Duma, the journalist wrote, the Czar had destroyed any hope of obtaining reforms without violence.

In India, what finally lit the fuse was the breaking up of Bengal in 1905. Justified by administrative needs, this

*V*iceroy Lord Curzon photographed with the maharaja of Patiala, a state that then had a little more than 1,500,000 inhabitants. The British let more than four hundred princely states survive, large and small. Nominally independent, they were actually controlled by British officials (the "residents").

partition was ordered by the viceroy, Lord Curzon, who aimed to break the backbone of this vast and turbulent administrative district. Bengal was divided into two presidencies: the western one (which included Bihar and Orissa), with Calcutta, and the eastern one, joined to Assam, with Dakha. The Muslims came to be the majority in East Bengal. This division remained viable only for a few years; it would be abolished in 1908. But in the meantime, Lord Curzon's decision would cause an outbreak of great violence.

Suddenly a *swadeshi,* or boycott movement, took hold. It was a total boycott of English goods, and stimulated the autonomous production of necessary items.

Clamorous strikes and student demonstrations were held. Under pressure from Tilak and the other "extremist" leaders, even the moderates joined in condemning the division of Bengal, and demonstrated in favor of the boycott. First in 1905, and then, more determinedly, in 1907, a wave of terrorism was unleashed which was destined to last, though with waning intensity, till 1917. Terrorist attacks gave rise, as usual, to waves of police and judicial repression, followed by a terrorist response.

The political violence which had sprung up in Bengal spread rapidly in other states, though its epicenter remained in Bengal. Terrorism did not spring from a centralized organization, but rather from numerous groups, often in competition with one another. Some were inspired by traditionalist Hinduism, some by anarchism. They tried to instigate armed conflict by encouraging the mutiny of Indian soldiers and seeking help from England's enemies; or at any rate, they wanted to paralyze the machinery of government through violent action, including the murder of British civil servants.

A police sentry, circa 1930, has just captured a small cobra, which he is holding in his left hand.

Between 1907 and 1917, sixty-four people were assassinated, mostly judges, military officers, and high functionaries; but at least in one case, there were chance victims (two English women were killed by mistake). Numerous robberies occurred, with the aim of obtaining weapons and money for the movement. Repression was fierce: all forms of assembly, even peaceful ones, were prohibited; newspaper editors and journalists were condemned for crimes of opinion; there were mass deportations, especially of youths, and severe sentencing for sedition and conspiracy. Tilak himself was sent to prison.

Repression and the decline of the movement drove into exile many young revolutionaries who had escaped conviction in court. Some went to London, and others to North America, where they mixed in with the populous communities of Indian emigrant laborers along the Pacific coast, from British Columbia to California. Even Japan received exiles, as well as Switzerland and other European countries. Gandhi himself would meet some of them.

Chapter 2

GANDHI: YOUTH, STUDIES, SOUTH AFRICA

THE FAITH, EXPERIENCE AND DEDICATION OF THE FATHER OF NON-VIOLENCE ARE FORGED IN HIS NATIVE GUJARAT, IN LONDON ("CAPUT MUNDI"), AND IN HIS EARLY STRUGGLES IN FAVOR OF THE DIGNITY OF INDIAN IMMIGRANTS IN SOUTH AFRICA

Mohandas Karamchand Gandhi was born in 1869 at Porbandar, a little town on the west coast of India, in the region of Gujarat. Gujarat could boast of ancient commercial and maritime traditions, which made it a lively cultural and religious crossroads as well.

Gandhi's family belonged to a subgroup of the third great caste of India, the merchant caste, or *banya*. In fact, both his father, Karamchand, and his grandfather, occupied the post of *diwan* during a total period of 28 years — first for the local maharaja, and then in a nearby princely state. The *diwan* was somewhat comparable to a prime minister; the family, then, was relatively well-off, but not of a high caste: and this position differentiated Gandhi from most of the great nationalist leaders of India, nearly all of them Brahmins (Gokhale, Tilak, Nehru). His was also a deeply religious family, but — it is important to note — one of great tolerance. They practiced Vishnuite Hinduism, but many of their friends were Muslims, including young Mohandas's best school friend. At high school, the most important teacher was a Zoroastrian Parsi. Gandhi's mother, Putlibal, had been raised in an ascetic sect preaching the need for charity, and prohibiting the consumption of drugs, tobacco, meat, and alcohol. The adviser Gandhi himself most closely heeded was a Jainist monk. Jainism is the religion — or, some would say, the branch of Hinduism — that has most

Gandhi in an 1893 photo, shortly after his arrival in South Africa. A young lawyer aware of his rights and duties as a citizen of the British Empire, during this period of his life Gandhi wears clothes adapted to his role and social rank.

assiduously developed the concept and commandment of *ahimsa*, the prohibition against harming any living creature; it advocates natural medicine and eating habits, chastity, and limiting possessions.

At first sight, we seem to find gathered about this boy many of the tendencies that will typify the mature Gandhi. And yet it would be erroneous to think in terms of a "clerical" upbringing, as we tend to say, or of a precociously "Gandhian" Gandhi. Anyone who reads his

autobiography, which is the main source for understanding the early part of his life, can discover therein a slightly unexpected Gandhi, even a mischievous one, who in the company of a naughty companion runs off to try smoking cigarettes, and eating meat, in a comically clandestine and sinful atmosphere. A very normal boy, who actually stands out a bit in his criticism of popular religious "superstitions."

At the age of thirteen he followed the Indian tradition of arranged childhood marriage, by marrying a girl his age, Kasturbai. His first son, born two years later, died almost immediately. Later, Mohandas and Kasturbai would have four other sons: Harilal, Manilal, Ramdas, and Devadas. When Gandhi was sixteen his father died, after a long period of illness. At the moment of the father's death young Gandhi was not at his side, but in bed with his wife. He would thereafter carry a heavy burden of guilt over this.

The home where Gandhi was born at Porbandar, a seaside town in the state of Gujarat.

In London

After finishing high school, Gandhi rather stubbornly insisted on going to London for his university studies. With the help of his mother and the Jainist monk, he overcame the hostility of his caste and left for London, after promising his mother to abstain from eating food of animal origin, drinking alcohol, and sexual contact with women. He reached London and began to study law — indeed, he was to become a lawyer.

His early days in London were very trying. It was difficult to get around in London, for a young Indian torn between two worlds. On one hand, Gandhi saw himself as a citizen of the British Empire: he *wanted* to be a citizen of the British Empire. He dressed like a perfect English gentleman, he studied, he even took dancing and violin lessons. On the other hand, he was a Hindu, observing his prohibitions, his rules, the promises made to his mother. It was above all the need to respect a vegetarian diet that made him ill at ease in that new environment. His life changed when he discovered a vegetarian restaurant, met some "militant" vegetarians, and joined their society, becoming quite an active member. His first published writings of which we know appeared in the review, *The Vegetarian*; and his first public speech took place during a meeting against cruelty to animals. This first experience in public speaking caused him a great deal of nervousness: even later, it would be very hard for him to overcome his nerves in public. Even when he got used to dealing with big crowds, he would never be a brilliant and impassioned orator, but rather a calm and controlled communicator, whose success rose from the force of reason and of his innate charismatic qualities.

*G*andhi's parents: his mother, Putlibal, and his father, Karamchand.

In London Gandhi also met several theosophists — members of a society that strove to intensify relations between East and West. They introduced him to the Bhagavad Gita, an ancient text most highly venerated by Hinduism; it would become Gandhi's favorite book. And here we observe a curious paradox: when the eighteen-year-old Gandhi left for England, he was virtually an atheist; he was a vegetarian simply out of family tradition; culturally, he felt more at ease as a citizen of the British Empire than he did as an Indian. But when he left London, he had discovered his roots, found his identity. He had approached the Hindu classics with attention and respect. He had become an ardent vegetarian.

East and West

This is an enlightening story for those interested in the problem of East-West relations. In nineteenth-century England — as well as in many other countries, from the United States to Russia — a number of movements developed which shared an aversion to industrial civilization, and to the loss of humanity in personal relationships which resulted from its materialism.

Some of these movements' protagonists felt nostalgia for a pre-capitalist society; others were socialists. They included pacifists, advocates of women's liberation, enthusiasts who had rediscovered nature and the body, founders of rural communes where new social relations could be experimented with, proto-ecologists; in some way, they all lived before their time. Some names? John Ruskin, Edward Carpenter, and William Morris in England; Leo Tolstoy above all (these figures are all, in some measure, Tolstoyan); in the United States, Henry David Thoreau, whose famous *Walden* told of his two-year experience in an isolated cabin in the forest, where he tried to live in solitude and harmony with nature. Such movements were overshadowed in their time by a different type of criticism of capitalist civilization: that of the workers' movements inspired by Marxism. All these movements resisting industrialization remained minority groups, with few but faithful followers who were ready to spring up again and spread their word. Now, the curious thing

Gandhi as a student in London, aged 21.

is this: all or nearly all the protagonists of this story were also admirers of Asia, particularly of Indian culture. They read and wrote books on India; they traveled there. It is with this world of the West's "heretics" that Gandhi came into contact in London (maintaining ties with them in the years that followed): either by meeting some of them personally, or by reading their works. And it was this world that gave Gandhi back his identity or, at any rate, greatly assisted him in recovering it.

Such an experience demands a complex vision of the relationship between East and West. East and West are not closed to each other; the relationship of the two is not one-way in either direction, but rather circular. At any rate, that is the way Gandhi considered it: an open relationship, founded on tolerance and respect for diversity. A respect not meant, however, to silence criticism of those aspects of one's own and others' cultures which seem inhuman and oppressive.

Again, young Gandhi in London in a photo of 1890 depicting him (lower right) with other members of the Vegetarian Society.

Gandhi in front of his Johannesburg office in 1905. The woman is Miss Schlesin, a secretary of Russian origin.

In South Africa

By 1891 Gandhi was a young lawyer. He was not yet what one would call a nationalist; he continued to consider himself a loyal British subject. Grievous news greeted him upon his return to the homeland: his mother, to whom he had been so close, had died while he was away. He started looking for employment, but with little success. He hardly seemed cut out to be a lawyer. Then something happened that would change all the rest of his life. An Indian firm doing business in South Africa asked him to travel there in order to represent it in a civil suit against another Indian firm. In May of 1893 Gandhi went to South Africa and started his work.

But immediately, during a train journey from Durban to Pretoria, he had occasion to confront the racism practiced by white South Africans. He was in a first-class compartment, as well befitted a lawyer who had studied in London. A "white" saw him and called the conductor. When Gandhi refused to move to a third-class seat, he was brutally thrown off the train in the dead of night, at the Maritzburg station. Later, Gandhi would remember that night as a decisive event in his life story: the occasion for a painful awakening.

At that time in South Africa there were about 100,000 Indians: merchants, unskilled laborers, domestic servants, miners, and above all, peasants who had been sent over from India to work as indentured servants on plantations, and who toiled in conditions of near slavery. Soon, Gandhi saw how oppressed his compatriots were by the whites: deprived of their rights as citizens, pushed to the edges of society, subjected to harassment of every sort. For instance, they were excluded from the better hotels, which were reserved for Europeans. They were forced to live in separate quarters, in squalid suburbs. They were not allowed to go out at night, or even walk on the sidewalk.

After about a year's stay in South Africa, Gandhi had terminated his work: the trial had ended (through his merit) in a compromise satisfactory to both sides. He was just about to leave India when some friends of his persuaded him to take up the cause of Indian immigrants in South Africa. His life was at a crossroads. He had gone to South Africa with the intention of stay-

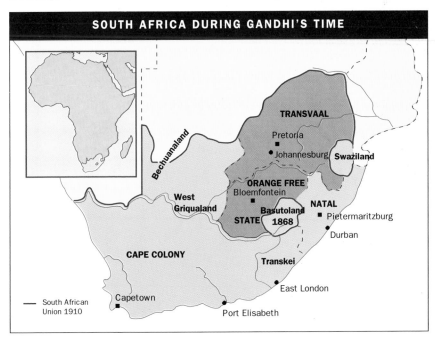

SOUTH AFRICA DURING GANDHI'S TIME

When Gandhi arrived in 1893, South Africa was divided up into four territories. Cape Colony and Natal, British Crown colonies, were accorded a wide measure of autonomy. Transvaal and the Orange Free State were independent republics, even though their independence was threatened by the British (who had an-

nexed them to the Cape Colony for several years). They had been founded about half a century before, by the Dutch — the "Boers." After the bloody war between the British and the Boers from 1899 to 1902, Transvaal and the Orange Free State lost their independence, and were joined to the Cape Colony and Natal. Together, the four

states formed the Union of South Africa, which in 1910 obtained the status of a dominion within the British Empire. At that time, approximately 123,000 Indian immigrants resided there — i.e., 1.3 percent of the total population. Indians were most numerous in Natal, and less so in Transvaal and the Cape Colony. ■

ing only a few months; he would remain there, apart from brief intervals, for over twenty years. And in South Africa he would elaborate many of the ideas that would lead him to become the *Mahatma*, the Great Soul — the most respected and inspiring political leader of India.

Twenty Years of Struggles
Right from the beginning of his stay in South Africa, Gandhi had become involved with the problems of his compatriots: for example, he had obtained permission for Indians to travel first class, if dressed properly. But most importantly, he had begun to gather together groups of Indians, organize them, speak to them. He strove to convince them that they could oppose

abuses with serene dignity, rather than passively accepting them.

At the moment when Gandhi decided to remain in South Africa, a new law in the state of Natal took away the Indians' voting rights. (Until then, at least a few Indians had been qualified to vote on the basis of their education and census classification, since they were citizens of the British Empire.) Another law, which was meant to put a halt to immigration, threatened to deal a serious blow to the Indian community. According to this law, an immigrant worker could no longer remain in South Africa as a free laborer, once his indenture period had expired, unless subjected to very trying conditions: he would have to sign a new two-year inden-

An episode of the Anglo-Boer War on November 15, 1899. Soldiers of the 2nd battalion of the Royal Fusiliers of Dublin are boarding a train which will shortly be attacked and derailed by the Boers. Among the British taken prisoners by the Boers on this occasion was Winston Churchill, a young war correspondent, who nonetheless managed to escape and return to be among the British two months later.

ture contract, or else pay a tax exorbitant in relation to his salary.

During the years that followed, new discriminatory measures struck the Indian community. Indians were prohibited from moving about freely within South Africa. In 1906, the Transvaal government imposed mortifying forms of administrative and police control, such as the obligation for each Indian, male or female, above

the age of eight years, to be registered, having their fingerprints taken like criminals; anyone who failed to comply could be deported, imprisoned, or made to pay a heavy fine. Later — again, in Transvaal — a law pronounced that only those marriages celebrated in a Christian ceremony were valid. Hindus, Muslims, and Parsis suddenly found their marriages legally nonexistent, and their children illegitimate.

On all of these fronts, Gandhi waged a relentless series of battles for nearly two decades. His struggle led him to prison twice, but nevertheless he led the Indian community to acquire a strong cultural and political consciousness, though at the price of great sacrifice.

From Petitions to *Satyagraha*

The maturing of Gandhi's ideas and his methods of struggle went hand in hand with that of the entire Indian community. At first, Gandhi confronted the problems of Indians in South Africa with legal methods: with petitions and press campaigns showing the hypocrisy of whites, their betrayal of their own principles. He gathered the uncertain and the dispersed into an organized community, giving them a forum for their

discussions: as early as 1894, the Indian Congress of Natal was born, based on that of the mother country.

At the same time, Gandhi insisted on his loyalty toward the British Empire. He even went so far as to organize the participation of Indians (though only in the role of stretcher-bearers and medics) alongside the British during two successive wars, fought first against the Boers (1899) and then against the Zulus (1906). If Indians were to enjoy the rights of citizenship he believed that they could not shirk its duties.

Many years later, Gandhi himself analyzed that formative period in a highly articulate way. He had been, he said, a very active reformer and writer of petitions. But he was forced to admit that reason was not sufficient. He was forced to choose between either joining the violent protest movement or finding another method to resolve the crisis and stop injustice. He thus conceived the idea of refusing to obey discriminatory laws, even in the face of imprisonment. This was the "moral equivalent of war"; though at the time he still tended to consider himself a loyalist, convinced as he was that, all in all, the actions of the British Empire were for the "good of India and humanity."

Little by little, Gandhi began to put into practice and perfect the techniques of passive resistance and civil

Gandhi (second row, fifth from the left) with the members of his special Indian ambulance corps, 1899.
Left, a print showing Indian medics at work during the Boer War. Le Petit Journal, end of the 19th century.

"I want to see God face to face. God I know is Truth. For me the only means of knowing God is non-violence — ahimsa *— love."*

Young India, *April 1924*

disobedience inspired, among other sources, by the American, Thoreau, whose books he read while in prison. For example, he responded to the compulsory registration of Indians by publicly burning the certificates, thus risking the blows of the police, and imprisonment. Gandhi persuaded his compatriots to swear a solemn oath: they would not submit to unjust laws, even if this refusal were to cause them imprisonment, physical pain, or death. But at the same time, they swore to reject the use of any violence against their enemies.

The following step would be decisive for the rest of Gandhi's life. It was taken in 1907, the year that Gandhi elaborated a theory and method of struggle which he named *satyagraha*, literally "power of truth." Its deep meaning, as Gandhi would write a few years later, is adherence to truth, and therefore "the power of truth." He also defined it as the power of love or the power of the soul. In applying *satyagraha*, he said, he had discovered from the very first that the search for truth would never consent to the use of violence against one's enemy; the adversary must be led away from error through patience and understanding, because what looks like truth to one man may seem erroneous to another. And patience means willingness to suffer. Practically speaking, Gandhi's doctrine allowed that defending truth could mean suffering oneself, but not inflicting suffering on an adversary.

For years, South African Indians carried on their battle by following these principles. Under Gandhi's guidance they fought for their rights and their dignity. They went on strike and held peaceful marches in order to break the prohibition against freedom of movement. Both men and women courageously risked hunger, beatings, and imprisonment in the concentration camps in which they were enclosed; at one time, there were more than 2,500 Indians in jail.

This great struggle ended on June 30, 1914, with a pact signed by Gandhi and by Smuts, the Boer general who was then president of Transvaal (and future president of the Union of South Africa). The pact was a compromise satisfying some of the Indians' demands and, above all, recognizing their dignity. It recognized

Arrival of Indian immigrants in the port of Durban, in Natal, towards the end of the 19th century.

the validity of marriages celebrated according to non-Christian rites, and abolished the odious tax which had been required in order to remain as free men in South Africa after the termination of indenture. In turn, Indians agreed not to pass from one South African state to another without an identity card; only Indians born in South Africa were allowed to enter the Cape Colony freely. In addition, from 1920 on, the immigration of indentured Indian workers was abolished.

Decisive Years

The story of Gandhi's battle in South Africa, then, ended in a partial victory. But even though new discriminatory measures were implemented in the years that followed, that victory remained indelibly engraved in the historical memory of Indians — and not only those residing in South Africa. Moreover, Gandhi's twenty-year stint in South Africa constituted an authentic laboratory for his spiritual and political formation. For one thing, it modified his character. Shortly after receiving his law degree, he had been pathologically timid and introverted. As late as 1896, in Bombay, he was invited to speak at an assembly in favor of the South African Indians, but could not bring himself to read a speech that he had prepared beforehand (a local orator ended up reading it). Later, he overcame this weakness thanks to his extraordinary willpower and, above all, to the conviction that the importance of his mission should take precedence over any personal problem.

During the same years, Gandhi made important life choices. For example, in 1906 he made a solemn vow of *brahmacharya*, promising not only chastity, but continence and self-control in his eating habits, emotions, and language; a vow aspiring to the absence of desire and possession. This vow was meant to free him from

Gandhi sitting beside Gokhale, during the latter's visit to South Africa in 1912. With them are some members of the Indian community of South Africa, and collaborators of Gandhi. Gokhale (sitting in the front row, wearing glasses and a long white scarf) was then the leader of the moderates, and one of the most prestigious leaders of Congress. Gandhi revered him.

the bonds of money, pain, and pleasure — from the gifts of nature — so that he could dedicate all his energy to the cause that he had embraced.

In South Africa, Gandhi was not only a lawyer and political leader. He worked as a journalist, founding and, to a large extent, writing the newspaper *Indian Opinion* (just as he would later do in India, with *Young India* and *Harijan*). He founded two rural communities: the first in 1904, at Phoenix, a farm which lay a few miles from Durban, and to which he moved the newspaper's printing press; the second, near Johannesburg, in 1910 (Gandhi called this Tolstoy Farm, in honor of the Russian writer). Everyone on those farms did manual work, beginning with Gandhi himself, regardless of caste, education, or economic condition. Gandhi also acted as doctor for his compatriots. He had always nurtured a great interest in the care of the body; he studied Western medicine and wrote several books about natural therapies. During the years when he was politically organizing the South African Indians, he also took care to educate them, criticize their faults, and urge them to abandon their prejudices and superstitions and comply with good health norms. This ten-

dency would remain a constant in Gandhi during the decades to follow: that is, he would always attempt to unite the struggle for independence with the social and cultural transformation of his compatriots.

Gandhi (fifth from the right, sitting in the center) photographed together with some of the first guests of the Tolstoy Farm.

On departing for India in 1914, Gandhi gave Smuts a pair of his sandals, which the Boer general religiously saved, out of respect and admiration for a man who had been a tough but loyal adversary.

The South African years had not only been years of success for Gandhi, but also ones of great sacrifice, risk, and bitter experience. He had faced imprisonment, with serenity. In 1897, as soon as he stepped off the steamship that had carried him to Durban from India, he risked being lynched by a group of whites. He was saved by the quick intervention of the wife of the police superintendent, who shielded him while brandishing her umbrella. Both in this and in similar cases, Gandhi refused to denounce his aggressors. Later, he was to become the target of three other attempts on his life, the last of which would cause his death.

Nor did his leadership over the South African Indians assert itself without accident and contradiction: in 1907 he was victim to a violent attack by two Pathans (a community from northeast India); they accused him of showing an excessively conciliatory attitude toward the authorities. Above all, in South Africa Gandhi came face to face with the problem of violence, even within his own community, where many advocated tougher methods of struggle. Gandhi also had to face this problem in London, where he traveled in 1909.

Gandhi (on the left) converses with H. Kallenbach, G. Isaac, and Mrs. Polak at the Maritzburg station in December, 1913, after being released from prison. The year before Gandhi had abandoned his European-style clothing in favor of a traditional Indian costume. He had also given up milk, and limited his diet to fresh or dry fruit.

Gandhi, then, stayed in South Africa from 1893 till 1914. But he made several journeys during that period. He went to India twice, in 1896 and in 1901..The first journey was to fetch his family; he returned to England with his wife, two sons, and a nephew. But he also took advantage of his travels to publicize the cause of the Indians in South Africa, and to make contact with the leaders of Congress, including Tilak and, more importantly, Gokhale, whom he revered. Word had reached India of his battles in South Africa; people listened attentively when he spoke. In 1901, he was able to speak at the annual session of Congress.

Two other journeys, in 1906 and 1909, led Gandhi to London. There, too, he met with political figures, spread information about the situation of South Africa's Indians, and requested help and solidarity.

Gandhi's Authors

Gandhi's experience in South Africa was decisive: not only in his political, family, and social life, but also for his culture and religion. Two of his most faithful collaborators there, Henry Polak and Hermann Kallenbach, were secular Jews. Gandhi had occasion to meet exponents of diverse religions and denominations, including Christian ones; he held long discussions with them, and some tried to convert him. It was a Jainist poet and thinker from Bombay, Raychandbhai, who confirmed Gandhi in the faith of his fathers.

Gandhi met him on his return to India from England, and continued to correspond with him from South Africa, until the poet's premature death. In his autobiography, Gandhi wrote that only once in his life had he come close to choosing a personal guru: yes, Raychandbhai. He considered him "the best Indian of his time," and freely acknowledged his debt to the Jain. If his Christian friends in London had awakened in him "the thirst for a religious quest," Raychandbhai had taught him that religion was essentially the control of one's own spirit, and liberation from any attachment or aversion to people or things.

It was principally during his South African years that

The last photo of Gandhi in Durban, before he left South Africa for good. Mohandas is sitting beside his wife, Kasturbai, and the two are surrounded by many friends.

Gandhi became acquainted with writers whom he would consider masters for the rest of his life: Ruskin, Thoreau, Carpenter, Tolstoy. In 1904 he read Ruskin's *Unto this Last*, a book identifying the individual good with the common good, and speaking of the importance of work as the cornerstone of life; for Ruskin, all types of work have equal dignity and value, whether they be intellectual or manual, noble or humble. In 1907, Gandhi read Thoreau's "On the Duty of Civil Disobedience," and was struck by its central theme: one's duty to refuse to obey a country's laws if one believes them to be unjust. Two years later, while in London, he read a volume written by the idealistic socialist, Edward Carpenter: *Civilisation: Its Cause and Cure*. He found it "enlightening," excellent in its analysis of civilization. An advocate of the return to a simple life in harmony with nature, Carpenter condemned modern civilization as degrading and corrupting; like Ruskin, he exalted the joy of manual work, which industrialism had separated from the creative project.

Raychandbhai (Rajchandra Ravjibhai Mehta, 1868–1901) was a poet, mystic, and Bombay jewelry seller who exercised great influence over Gandhi. The two met in 1891, on Gandhi's return to India from London, and they kept up a correspondence until Raychandbhai's premature death.

However, the author that struck Gandhi more than any other was Tolstoy. All during the rest of his life, Gandhi would recognize his debt to the Russian writer. He probably read Tolstoy for the first time during the London years of his youth, when he greatly admired the author's ideas and work. But his first great encounter with Tolstoy dates back to 1894, in South Africa, when a friend gave him a copy of *God's Reign is Within You*. Gandhi's reading of it left an indelible impression on him. He felt for the book and its author the same admiration that he had held for the Sermon on the Mount. He found in it an admonition against responding to evil with violence, an exhortation to love one's neighbor and practice pacifism, and a confirmation of the ancient Indian commandment (Jainist, in particular) of *ahimsa*. He also found a brief story of the forerunners of non-

John Ruskin (left) and his painter friend, William Holman Hunt, in an 1894 image captured by one of the greatest portrait photographers of the late Victoria age, Frederick Hollyer. Ruskin was then seventy-five.

violence, and a catalogue of its advocates and "militants" at that time: from the Quakers to Tom Paine, from the American abolitionists to the Russian *duchobors*.

In other books by Tolstoy which he read in the years that followed, Gandhi was led to agree more and more adamantly with the Russian's distillation of Christianity — and of every religious faith — to the commandment to love one's neighbor; the aspiration toward a profound moral rebirth of man; a highly critical attitude toward progress, science, luxury, and wealth, as well as toward the city, a place of alienation and destruction of man's deepest values.

1909 and *Hind Swaraj*

The year 1909 turned out to be very important in Gandhi's life. His journey to London dramatically awakened him to the problem of extremism. A few days before his arrival, the English capital had been thrown into chaos by a political assassination: a young Indian had killed an important functionary in the Ministry for Indian Affairs, along with an Indian physician who had tried to shield him from the shots. Shortly afterwards, during a public debate, Gandhi found himself face-to-face with a leader of the extremists, Savarkar. He was deeply impressed by the growing

GANDHI AND TOLSTOY

In 1909, Leo Tolstoy was eighty-one years old, and he was famous all over the world, not only for his great novels and short stories, but also for his role as thinker, religious man, and radical pacifist. His ideas — which can be summed up as the resistance to evil through love — had led him to clash several times with the Orthodox Church and the Czars. In his house at Jasnaja Poljana he received visits and kept up correspondence with people from all over the world. Members of highly varied schools of thought and religious creeds all venerated him. Gandhi was only forty years old, and although he had already conducted memorable battles in South Africa, his notoriety was still limited (outside South Africa) to a few groups in India and England.

That year, while answering the invitation of an Indian nationalist extremist, Tolstoy wrote and published a long *Letter to a Hindu*. It contained many ideas that seemed written to please Gandhi: the criticism of modern civilization as purely materialistic; criticism of violent action and terrorism as methods of struggle; emphasis on the responsibility of Indians themselves for their subjugation to the British; the need for Indians to begin their struggle against the

British with an intense effort of spiritual renewal. Gandhi already knew and appreciated the ideas that Tolstoy had developed after his "conversion" in the early 1880s. When he read the *Letter to a Hindu*, he decided to write to its author describing the situation of the Indians of Transvaal. Tolstoy

was moved on receiving Gandhi's letter (he wrote as much in his Diary) and answered immediately. He permitted Gandhi to republish the *Letter to a Hindu* in serial form in *Indian Opinion*. After a while, Gandhi sent Tolstoy his book, *Hind Swaraj*, which had just been published. Tolstoy greatly appreciated the book. At first, he showed a slightly condescending, paternal attitude; but his interest in Gandhi and South Africa increased considerably after reading *Hind Swaraj*. Seven letters were exchanged between the two most representative figures of pacifism in the twentieth century: four written by Gandhi, and three by Tolstoy. The correspondence

was interrupted by Tolstoy's death in 1910. Gandhi had already heard the news of the writer's death when he received Tolstoy's last letter: the longest and densest one of all, an authentic manifesto on the refusal of all violence, containing open acknowledgment of the non-violent struggle of Indians in the Transvaal. Gandhi acknowledged his debt to Tolstoy for the rest of his life; he studied his works and made them better known, and kept up correspondence with "Tolstoyans." When Gandhi was killed, Tolstoy's daughter, Tatyana, wrote Nehru a fine letter from Rome, where she lived, containing a vain request to pardon the assassins: "Gandhi, who liked to declare himself a disciple of Leo Tolstoy, and my father, would raise their voices, if they could, to prevent an act of violence from following on the crime committed by the two assassins...." ∎

On the right, Gandhi in a satyagrahi costume in a photo from the last South African period. In the following years Gandhi's clothing would become modified several times again, becoming more and more simple and poor. The staff would remain, both as symbol and concrete instrument aiding him in his protest marches.

influence exercised by such figures and their ideas.

During his London stay, Gandhi was disappointed by the outcome of his political talks. He was even more disappointed by the sight which the metropolis presented to his eyes, and which would lead him to elaborate his radical criticism of the false values of modern civilization. Matured by his experiences and by his readings of Tolstoy, Ruskin, and Carpenter, this radical criticism found expression in a booklet written in dialogue form, completed in a flash of inspiration: *Hind Swaraj*, or *Indian Home Rule*. It was published in Gujarati in 1909, and in English the following year.

Hind Swaraj launches a series of bitter accusations against modern civilization: against the machine, against science, against a medicine, which has reduced man to slavery, dehumanizing him and alienating him from nature and from the values of the spirit. Gandhi dreamed of opposing this civilization by returning to the spinning wheel and to the crude hoe of ancient times. The real conflict existing today, he held, was not between Indians and the British, or between East and West, but between two different forms of civilization: the slow, peaceful, patriarchal one of traditional India (but also, he argued, of pre-industrial Europe), and the madly frenetic, convulsive, selfish, and materialistic one of modern Europe (but also of that part of India which Europe had by then contaminated).

This disturbing book, published in an amazing number of editions up to our day, was openly criticized by several of India's moderate leaders, such as Gokhale, and ignored by others, such as Nehru. Gandhi never disowned it: he merely limited himself, many years lat-

er, to pointing out that it contained a sort of ideal life model, a noble long-term project, destined to adapt to the historical timetable of politics.

The modern reader may find *Hind Swaraj* irritating in its uncompromising radicalism, but it still has the power to transmit messages relevant today. In this booklet there is a sentence which effectively (and disturbingly) sums up one aspect of Gandhian thought: "We say then that the non-beginning of a thing is supreme wisdom." This sentence can be interpreted as an example of a purely conservative attitude, but also as a sign of deep respect for natural and cultural balance: of values such as slowness, which, arguably, we need to rediscover today. But *Hind Swaraj* and other writings and letters of Gandhi in the same period also reflect the decisive step taken in the evolution of

"We say then that the non-beginning of a thing is supreme wisdom."

his thought. Above all else, Gandhi was confronting the problem of India for the first time: he took this upon himself as his inevitable mission. He almost seemed to be saying that the very battles waged by the Indians of South Africa could not find true victory without extending them to India itself.

Gandhi spoke both to the moderates and to the extremists. To the former, he insisted that the time for respectful petitions was over: it was necessary to avoid any elitist temptation in order to communicate with the masses of India, who otherwise would fall into the hands of the extremists. To the latter, he said that it was not sufficient to fight the rulers in order to replace them in leading a country built by imitating their homeland. A victory attained through violence, he continued, would bring the violent to power: nothing could guar-

Gandhi speaks at a farewell assembly in South Africa, 1914.

antee that government by Indians would be better than government by the British. If it was true that by now, Indians needed to resort to force, this could only be the force of the truth: non-violence. It would be necessary to turn to the masses, not in order to communicate a message of violence and terror, but to help them rediscover their own history, their own ethics, the peaceful customs of antiquity, and the forgotten languages. Only in this way could Indian independence avoid rising on a rotten foundation. Independence was not only meant to bring about political change, but also to be a great victory on behalf of civilization.

The Gandhi of 1909 held within himself the seed of

KEY WORDS IN

Among the key words in Gandhi's language, the first and foremost is without a doubt **Ahimsa**, which literally means "non-killing." An ancient word dating back to the origins of Jainism, ahimsa for Gandhi meant "that you may not offend anybody: you may not harbor an uncharitable thought... To one who follows this doctrine, there is no room for an enemy."

Aparigraha, on the other hand, indicates non-possession, the renunciation of material goods which are not strictly necessary, and detachment from necessary ones. The observance of this principle, wrote Gandhi, leads to a progressive "simplification of life." And again: "Love and exclusive possession can never go together."

Brahmacharya is the vow of chastity, of sexual conti-

nence. But in Gandhi, it takes on a wider meaning. It includes non-possession, the observance of particularly frugal natural diets, psychological and physical self-discipline, control over one's passions, and preservation of one's vital energy in order to dedicate oneself entirely to the search for truth, and service to others.

Satyagraha, or the "force of truth," is a term coined by Gandhi by modifying a suggestion by a relative, in order to indicate his theory of non-violence. The term is widely discussed in this chapter.

Sarvodaya, or "common good, welfare of all," is the term that Gandhi adopted in translating the title of a book by Ruskin. It was later used to designate both the group of social initiatives presented in his "construction project," and an ideal of non-violent socialism founded

on the popular mobilization of individuals' energy, and on a fair distribution of wealth.

Swadeshi is not only the use of Indian products (especially textiles) instead of imported ones. It also refers to everything that is near: the spirit within that brings us to use the elements of our immediate surroundings, and reserve our attention for them, to the "exclusion of more distant places." But the concept of swadeshi, "like any other good thing," might become lethal if turned into a fetish. To reject foreign products simply because they are foreign, and continue to waste national time and money in order to sustain manufactured products which are inappropriate for the country, would be criminal madness — a negation of the spirit of swadeshi. A true follower of swadeshi will never nurture hate for the great leader of India's fight for independence he would become, although many years would pass before he could assume this role.

At the root of his new attitude was his need to meet the challenge represented by the extremists. The radical coherence of his theory of non-violence sprang from an acute awareness of the immense potential for violence present in Indian society, and from the will to oppose it. In 1909, Gandhi came face to face with that potential. And if it is true that in *Hind Swaraj*, as in many other writings, he claimed that violence was extraneous to Indian culture, he did so only because he intended to make a choice.

GANDHI'S LANGUAGE

the foreigner; he will never let himself be overcome by antagonism toward anyone living in the world. Swadeshi is not a cult of hate. It is a doctrine of generous altruism, which sinks its roots into the purest ahimsa, or love. ∎

The Transvaal march in Autumn, 1913, was the prelude to the final pact with Smuts, which led to Gandhi's finally leaving South Africa. Intending to protest against the barriers put up by the Transvaal government against the immigration of Indians, Gandhi left Newcastle and headed towards Volksrust together with 2,000 marchers, who crossed the border without the required certificates. Both Gandhi and his main collaborators did everything possible to go to prison, accusing themselves or each other.

Chapter 3

GANDHI:
SATYAGRAHA IN **I**NDIA

HAVING RETURNED TO INDIA, GANDHI BECOMES THE MOST WIDELY-ADMIRED LEADER ON THE COUNTRY'S ROAD TO INDEPENDENCE. THE DOCTRINE OF NON-VIOLENCE, THOUGH BESET BY PROBLEMS AND CONFLICT, MAKES INDIA UNIQUE AMONG COUNTRIES FIGHTING FOR THEIR FREEDOM.

Having concluded his pact with Smuts, Gandhi sailed for London on July 18, 1914, leaving South Africa for the last time. In London, where he arrived two days after the start of the First World War, he dedicated himself to organizing an ambulance squad, as he had already done in South Africa, made up of Indian students. Later, in 1918, he would accept the viceroy's request to publicize the war effort in order to recruit Indians. The war of 1914–1918 was the last occasion on which Gandhi pushed his loyalty to the Empire that far (in so doing, he attracted the criticism of several important exponents of international pacifism — then, and later on as well).

At any rate, in December of 1914, health reasons led Gandhi to sail for India, on what was to be his final return to the homeland. Soon after arriving in India, Gandhi founded an ashram in Ahmedabad that was to become his most celebrated headquarters: the Sabarmati ashram. Soon afterwards, he granted admission there to the first family of untouchables, in a deeply meaningful gesture that provoked the hostility of some of his own followers, and ran the risk of losing the financial assistance that the community received from outside.

The ashram was at the same time a religious community, an experiment in coexistence, and a school for

Mahatma ("the Great Soul") is a very solemn name (it was Tagore who gave it to him). But the Indians more often addressed Gandhi with more familiar names: for example, Bapu *("Father"), which implies affectionate respect; or* Gandhiji, *or* Bapuji, *where the suffix "ji" adds a special sense of veneration.*

leaders where aspirants learned and practiced *satya-graha*, *brahmacharya*, aversion to any form of violence, non-fear, poverty, manual labor, and community prayer.

Gokhale, the Congress leader to whom Gandhi had been closest (and who would die in 1915 at just over fifty years of age), gave him a precious piece of advice shortly before his death. Gandhi had been away from India so long that, for the time being, he could not effectively throw himself into the political fray: he would do better to become acquainted with India — all of India, the true India, the India of many cities and a myriad of villages. So Gandhi spent much of 1916 journeying throughout India and Burma in third-class railway cars, wearing the traditional Indian costume. It was during one of those journeys that Gandhi visited the

Gandhi talking with villagers in 1916, during one of his trips across India.

famous poet, Rabindranath Tagore (who had won the Nobel Prize four years before); and it was Tagore who first called Gandhi *Mahatma*, the "Great Soul."

In 1917 Gandhi met Mahadev Desai, a Gujarati lawyer and writer 25 years of age, and appointed him as his secretary. Desai would remain by his side until Gandhi's death in 1942. The following year, Gandhi made the equally-important acquaintance of Vallabhbhai Patel, who was a Gujarati as well. Patel was willing to leave his successful law practice in order to follow

Gandhi. Later, he was to become one of the major leaders of Congress, and an eminent protagonist in India's struggle for independence. The woman poet, Sarojini Naidu, also became tied to Gandhi's cause, immediately after meeting him for the first time.

In the meantime, Gandhi's popularity continued to grow. Individuals, groups, and movements turned to him for guidance and support. Thus, between 1917 and 1918, Gandhi found himself participating in three important episodes of social combat. First, he helped to organize and lead the peasants' struggle in the district of Champaran, in Bihar, where for centuries they had been victims of a scandalous form of exploitation by the British indigo planters. Then he participated in a struggle over salary claims made by the textile workers of Ahmedabad (with whom he formed a non-violent labor union). On that occasion, Gandhi alternated his activity as union organizer with that of mediator between the workers and the textile entrepreneurs, in a rather complicated situation. The most powerful and influential entrepreneur was, in fact, a friend of Gandhi's, and had materially helped his *ashram*. One of the industrialist's sisters chose to side with Gandhi and the laborers. Not surprisingly, the conflict turned out to be bitter (so much so that Gandhi undertook an all-out hunger strike), and brought with it a crisis of conscience; but not one sufficient to make his personal sentiments prevail over his sense of justice. A few days after this matter was resolved, Gandhi traveled to the district of Kheda, in Gujarat, where the peasants were starving, oppressed by a harassing tax system; to them, too, he offered leadership and help.

Gandhi and Kasturbai in Bombay in 1915.

The first two of these conflicts ended with success, in traditional Gandhian style: that is, through more or less acceptable compromise. The peasant struggle in

Indian soldiers on the French front in 1917 and, on the right, posing on the steps of a pyramid in Egypt, in 1919, while waiting to board ship to return to the homeland. India's contribution to the war effort was very important. The permanent soldiers in the Indian army reached the considerable number of 1,200,000 men who suffered great losses while fighting on several fronts, from France to the Middle East. It was the Indian army, for example, that conquered Mesopotamia for the British. Besides being submitted to a kind of undeclared draft, Indians also had to contribute to the war effort financially. All this helps to explain why, in the years 1914–1918, the Indians had begun to hope increasingly for future recognition from Britain. They were to be disappointed.

Kheda had a less fortunate outcome, but was not totally defeated. All three episodes, at any rate, resonated throughout much of India. They consecrated Gandhi as a political leader, and confirmed his fame as an indomitable combatant and great organizer. They allowed him to experiment with his techniques of non-violent struggle in India for the first time, now applying them to generalized social battles, and not only civil rights. In at least one case, the Kheda matter, Gandhi's interlocutor and direct adversary had been the powerful British administration itself.

What is most important is that in all three cases Gandhi had achieved his chief aim: to liberate the Indian populace from the fear of power, by enhancing its political consciousness. And many Indian intellectuals, especially among the young, had hastened to join his side or had, at least, been struck by his example. They had understood the necessity of steadily approaching the poor masses of India, while coming to know and share their conditions, their needs, and their suffering. Therefore, the battles of Champaran, Ahmedabad, and Kheda laid down the foundations necessary to draw Indian political life, and the fight for independence itself, out into the open.

Satyagraha in India

Between 1917 and 1919, the British adopted measures which disappointed the aspirations of Indian nationalists, and which appeared, to say the least, contradictory.

In 1917, the Secretary of State for India, Lord Montagu, read to the House of Commons a declaration pre-announcing the development of forms of self-government. The following year, Montagu himself, together with Viceroy Chelmsford, presented a report which constituted the basis of the Government of India Act, promulgated in 1919. This law was intended to reform relations between provincial governments and the central government, by increasing the autonomy of the former. Moreover, it declared that provincial governments were to be formed in part by individuals appointed by the British (as in the past), and in part (here was the novelty) by elected representatives who would be responsible to the assemblies electing them. The management of numerous sectors, including education, health, public works, agriculture, and industry, would be transferred to these responsible Indian ministers.

In the eyes of the British, the Government of India Act was not an early sign pointing to independence — this was still out of the question — but an attempt to bind to the Empire a greater number of "educated" Indians, those belonging to the westernized elite, who were supposed to be faithful to Britain. However, by giving Indians greater opportunities for electoral self-expression, and permitting them to participate in pub-

Arrival in Bombay in December 1911 of George V, the first reigning sovereign of England to visit India, and his wife, Queen Mary. The imposing monument that we see here was built for the occasion; it combines references to the triumphal arches of ancient Rome with Indian architectural elements of the 16th century. Millions of travelers passed in both directions, beneath this arch, the "Gateway to India." In 1947, it also saw the passage of the last British troops, as they abandoned India after a colonial presence that had lasted, in various forms, for three and a half centuries. Thus, the Gateway to India became a symbol first of Great Britain's triumphs, and then, its decline.

lic administration, this early reform opened up new possibilities for action. Acceptable ones, in the opinion of some; too limited, in the eyes of others who had hoped for much greater concessions in exchange for the widespread participation of Indians in the war. After all was said and done, the British still reserved for themselves the management of the most crucial and important sectors, maintaining the governors' right of veto in all matters. A debate was therefore opened among Indians over the advisability of participating or not in the election of assemblies and local governments.

In 1919, while this debate was going on the legislative council of India issued a series of laws, the Rowlatt Acts, named after the judge who had presided over the commission proposing them. The Rowlatt Acts were none other than the peacetime extension of a series of measures taken during the war to repress terrorism. By maintaining special courts for political crimes, allowing arrests on the basis of mere suspicion, and detaining without trial for up to two years for those held to be potentially "subversive," these new laws gave legitimacy to the severe infringement of personal liberties. It is enlightening to read the brief formula with which these laws were summed up on the popular level: "no trial, no lawyer, no appeal." One can easily imagine the disappointment of many Indians on seeing the postwar period start off with such a repressive act — after so many hopes and promises.

The Rowlatt laws so shocked Gandhi that for the first time his loyalty to the Empire wavered perilously. He thought that any self-respecting people could and should refuse to submit to such impositions. Together with a group of his followers, he founded a *Satyagraha Sabha* (assembly of *satyagraha*), whose general headquarters in Bombay was quickly joined by numerous volunteers who were ready to serve as activists.

In early April (after informing the viceroy, as was his style) he launched a national campaign of non-violent non-cooperation. The campaign was to open with a *hartal*, that is, a national day of fasting and prayer, when all economic activity would be suspended. The *hartal* was proclaimed by Gandhi and his collaborators without the participation of Congress. The latter, in fact, was paralyzed by its internal divisions between moderates and extremists; during the First World War, it had split up into factions. For example, Tilak and Mrs. Annie Besant had temporarily left it in order to found a league for Home Rule, along the lines of the Irish one. Except for a few attempts on Tilak's part, Indian nationalism as it was expressed in Congress continued to have an elitist nature, both among the moderates and among the extremists, so that the masses were seldom involved.

However, in spite of the lack of support from Congress, the *hartal* was highly successful. Much of India was witness to strikes, shop closures, parades, mass demonstrations, and other forms of protest, such as the distribution of Gandhi's writings in open disobedience to the police authorities who had prohibited them. But in many localities, contrary to Gandhi's intentions, violence broke out on both sides. The violence culminated on April 13 in the massacre perpetrated by the

Annie Besant, née Wood (1847–1933), was a woman of many lives — and decidedly unusual ones, for her time. She married an Anglican minister, and soon separated; spoke out in favor of rationalistic and atheistic theories; became a socialist and organized one of the first women's strikes in London. For decades she was president of the Theosophic Society, founded in 1875, which joined a spiritualistic and occult tendency with the praiseworthy aim of spreading knowledge of Asian thought. Finally, her sympathy for Indian nationalism led her to become one of its leaders for some time; for example, she was President of the Calcutta Congress in 1917.

Indian police make arrests in Calcutta during the 1919 demonstrations. (p. 85): General Edward Dyer, responsible for the Amritsar massacre.

British at Amritsar, in Punjab, in which at least 379 Indians lost their lives.

After vainly trying to calm the fiery spirits, on April 18 Gandhi announced the temporary suspension of his campaign for non-cooperation. He accused himself of having made "an error the size of the Himalayas": he had "underestimated the forces of evil," the fury and violence of the Indian masses, and their lack of

APRIL 13, 1919:

The Amritsar massacre was perhaps the most shameful episode of British colonialism in India. The 1919 *hartal* was set by Gandhi for March 30. Its beginning was then postponed to April 6, but difficulties in communications caused demonstrations to break out on the original date. Almost immediately, non-violent demonstrations gave way in some cities to chaos and violence, often in reaction to brutal police intervention.

At Amritsar, the sacred city of the Sikhs, in Punjab, the demonstrations were peaceful at first. But following the arrest of two nationalist leaders they soon degenerated into episodes of violence: attacks against Europeans, assaults against banks and public offices, clashes with the police and army. Faced with the persistence of widespread social tension, Gandhi became persuaded that only his presence could defuse the bomb, and he set off for Punjab; but the British authorities did everything they could to block his way. They ended up forcing him onto a train and turning him back. On April 13, Brigadier-

General Edward Harry Dyer, who had arrived three days before in order to command the troops present at Amritsar, was informed that a crowd planned to gather at 4:30 in the afternoon in the Jallianwala Bagh. This was a square entirely closed in on all sides by buildings or walls: the only entrance was through a narrow alley. And so, at the established hour, 15-20,000 people gathered there. At that point, Dyer,

who had done nothing to prevent the demonstration, entered the square as well, together with fifty infantrymen and fifty gurkha armed only with knives. He had also brought with him two armored tanks, but they did not fit through the alley leading to the square. Dyer gave the order to shoot, with no forewarning.

As was later documented, the shooting lasted ten minutes, during which time 1,600 bul-

preparation in responding to the adversary's provocation with non-violence.

In the following months, Gandhi dedicated himself to teaching *satyagraha*, spreading his ideas in two weekly magazines put at his disposal by friends. The magazines were to become the official voice of his movement: *Young India* was written in English, and *Navajivan* (New Life) in Gujarati at first, and later, in

AMRITSAR MASSACRE

lets were shot at a crowd desperately trying to make an escape.

After it was over, according to information obtained by the Punjab government, 379 people lay on the ground, shot to death (400, according to a later commission of inquiry), along with about 1,200 wounded: proof of stunningly precise, ruthless shooting. The Congress Party carried out its own inquiry and came to the conclusion that there had been about 1,000 killed: many bodies had been taken away by family or friends. This elevated figure has not, however, been accepted by historians; they still tend to speak of "over 400 dead."

The Punjab disorders, further enflamed by the massacre, lasted several days more and brought more bloodshed. When facing a commission of inquiry, Dyer claimed he had wanted to "inflict punishment" and "produce a moral effect" throughout Punjab. He admitted he had ordered his men to aim where the crowd was thickest, and declared that he had not taken care of the wounded because none of them had asked him to do so. In the days preceding the

massacre, Dyer had already earned distinction in minor episodes, if we may call them that — for example, forcing all the Indian passersby to crawl on their bellies along a city street where an English woman missionary had been attacked. Later, he continued to defend his acts, without showing the least remorse. The commission of inquiry and the government of the viceroy, while criticizing Dyer for an "erroneous conception" of his duty, expressed recognition of his honesty and his conviction of being in the right, and credited him with saving Punjab from the danger of widespread rebellion. Lord Montagu, Secretary of State for India, expressed a harsher judgment. In the end, Dyer was forced to resign and called back to England, where he died in 1927, at the age of sixty-three. No measures were taken against the governor of Punjab, Sir Michael O'Dwyer, who had not hesitated to approve the general's actions. Dyer also received warm demonstrations of solidarity, both in India (where English women were particularly active in his favor) and in Eng-

land. He was presented with a sword studded with precious stones, and engraved with the words: "To the saviour of Punjab." The *Morning Post* sponsored a donation which raised £30,000 for his benefit. The House of Lords passed a resolution approving his actions, with 129 votes against 86. It is only fair to recall that when Dyer and O'Dwyer left the Punjab they had helped to taint with blood, they were sent off in solemn ceremony attended by high Sikh authorities and representatives of other religious communities, by rajas, princes, and conservative pro-British public figures. ■

86

Hindi as well. He began to participate more actively in the Congress Party, becoming its most influential leader during the year 1920. (That same year marked the death of Tilak, the prestigious "extremist" leader.)

During the last months of 1919, Gandhi faced a new struggle, which he embraced with joy, as it allowed him to unite Hindus and Muslims in a common battle. He became involved, this time, in the defense of the Caliphate. Until the outbreak of World War I, the Sultan of Constantinople had also performed the role (though it was by now only nominal) of Caliph, or "successor" to Muhammad and supreme leader of the entire Islamic community, from Morocco to Indonesia. When the Ottoman Empire entered the war alongside Germany against England, the Indian Muslims had felt torn between two loyalties. Several of their leaders (such as

A demonstration in Bombay during the non-cooperation campaign of 1921 which witnessed the momentary collaboration of Hindus and Muslims in defense of the Caliphate.
Photo by N.V. Virkar.

the Ali brothers) had openly sided with Turkey, and been arrested. Later, the British had tried to make amends by promising that they would guarantee the survival of the Caliphate, whatever events might come to pass.

But after the war had ended, when peace talks were under way, it soon became clear that the Ottoman Empire would be divided up into factions, and throughout the Muslim world people began to fear that England would not keep its promise. As it happened, it was a Muslim — Mustafa Kemal, holding the reins of power in Turkey — who would abolish the Caliphate just a few years later (1924). In doing so, he caused discomfort and frustration in the Muslim world, but did not awaken particularly clamorous reactions. But before that happened, the Caliphate question was cause for protest and demonstrations. From 1919 on,

Gandhi himself fought alongside the Muslims in defense of the Caliphate. He persuaded Congress to embrace this new cause, although its leaders, who were predominately Hindu, were initially reluctant. It was the Caliphate question itself that originated the movement for non-cooperation from 1920–1922 — the second great anti-British campaign. In addition, the struggle for independence was widened by the scandalously bland conclusions reached by the commission of inquiry on the Amritsar massacre: many Indians found these conclusions offensive.

In August of 1920, Gandhi published an article in *Young India* which made a great impression, entitled "The Law of the Sword." While confirming his conviction that non-violence is "infinitely superior" to violence, at the same time he declared that if he were forced to

Gandhi with Muslim leader Maulana Shaukat Ali in 1919, during the Caliphate movement.

choose between cowardice and violence, he would choose violence. Rather than becoming or remaining, out of cowardice, a victim to its own dishonor, it would be preferable for India to take up arms in defense of its honor.

Shortly afterwards, during a crowded, extraordinary session of Congress in Calcutta, Gandhi demanded "reparation" for the wrongs perpetrated in Punjab, as well as the defense of the Caliphate. Both aims were to be pursued through non-cooperation. Among the traditional leaders of Congress, Motilal Nehru (father of the future premier of independent India) clearly expressed his approval of *swaraj*, or self-government, and at the same time, sided with Gandhi's methods of protest. Others, such as the Muslim, Jinnah, the Bengali (and former advocate of extremism), Chittarajan Das, Lala Lajput Raj, and Annie Besant, took sides against non-cooperation, which they considered to be a risky, ineffective political instrument. Nonetheless, Gandhi won a wide majority of approval, so that during the following Congress session, held in December at Nagpur, he was able to present himself as the unquestioned leader of the independence movement. It was at Nagpur that Gandhi began the transformation of Congress from an exclusive club of intellectuals and notables, to a genuine political party having a popular base and building permanent legislative structures.

In accordance with Gandhi's proposal, which it passed, Congress made arrangements to form provincial, district, and village committees; these would be led by a pan-Indian committee of 350 members and an action committee of fifteen members — i.e., a permanent executive body governing alongside an annually-elected president. The first article of the statute de-

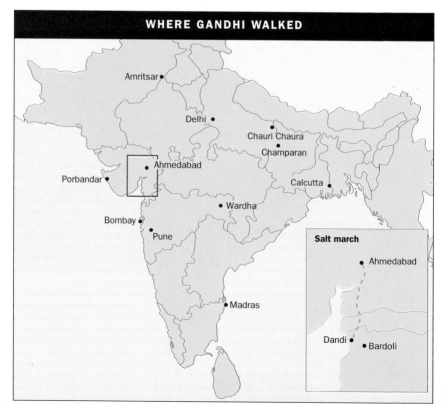

WHERE GANDHI WALKED

Amritsar

Delhi

Chauri Chaura

Champaran

Ahmedabad

Porbandar

Calcutta

Wardha

Bombay

Pune

Madras

Salt march

Ahmedabad

Dandi • Bardoli

clared that attainment of *swaraj* "through all legitimate and peaceful means" was the foremost aim. Other articles advocated unity of action between Hindus and Muslims; a war on untouchability, considered one of the cruelest scourges of India; and the promotion of *khadi*, fabric produced by hand-spinning local cotton. This time around, Das accepted Gandhi's proposals, as did Motilal Nehru, while the aristocratic Jinnah abandoned Congress, disgusted by a style of politics he found totally alien.

But Gandhi had convinced some of the most influential leaders of Congress of the rightness of mass *satyagraha*, as well as important Muslim leaders, including the Ali brothers, and Maulana Azad, who would remain among his most faithful collaborators for the rest of his life.

Non-cooperation was proclaimed, and the whole country was swept by a new wave of protest demon-

strations. Thousands of Indians resigned from the public offices they held and returned the honors and declarations they had received. Gandhi himself began the campaign by sending the viceroy the *Kaisar-i-hind* medal and the other decorations he had been given in South Africa for his participation in the Anglo-Boer War and the war against the Zulus. Schools, public administration,

Gandhi inaugurates a shop selling khadi *in Bombay, 1921.*

law courts, and legislative bodies were paralyzed. In many places national schools were instituted, and autonomous courts sprang up which practiced forms of private arbitration. During the elections of 1920, nearly two-thirds of the voters deserted the polls.

A boycott also hit British products, particularly textiles. In 1920, Gandhi decided to use only *khadi*. And in the following year, his clothing was to become part of his image all over the world: the *dhoti* (a strip of cloth knotted around his hips like short pants), and a sort of sheet, both of them white. with sandals on his feet. (The London years, in which he had dressed in Western-style elegance, were now part of the distant past.)

An encounter (Darjeeling, 1925) between Gandhi and one of the most prestigious leaders of Congress, the Bengali C.R. Das, who would suddenly die the same year.

In 1921, Gandhi made a vow to dedicate part of his time each day to spinning cotton by hand. More and more, he began trying to spread this custom among his compatriots. A few years before, an elderly widow had given him great joy by sending him an antique spinning wheel, which she had managed to find in a village. This was the *charkha*, which soon became one of the symbols of Congress. (Later, in stylized form, it would also appear on the Indian flag.)

The boycott against English goods reached both its real and symbolic climax, at the end of July of that year when Gandhi presided over a huge bonfire set to burn British fabrics in Bombay.

The viceroy and his government were initially taken by surprise by the non-cooperation campaign, whose effectiveness and popular appeal they had underestimated. They began to react with a series of repressive interventions which resulted mainly in increasing the tension. Arrests and summary trials intensified, especially following a visit to India by the Prince of Wales in November 1921. He was greeted in Bombay by a great

"The spinning wheel signifies India's national consciousness and represents the contribution each individual makes to the constructive work of the whole nation."

hartal of protest, followed by violent riots. In the early months of 1922, the Indian jails came to contain nearly 30,000 "non-cooperators": included among the prisoners were the two Nehrus, the Ali brothers, Muhammad and Shaukat, and Chittarajan Das.

As had happened in 1919, the country was swept by violent riots, which Gandhi and his followers were not always able to control. And once again, it was an episode of violence that made him declare the campaign closed.

In early 1922, reluctantly giving in to the pressure from some of his allies, he decided to take a further step in the campaign by instituting "total disobedience" at Bardoli, in the district of Surat (in his native state of Gujarat). This included the refusal to pay taxes. Gandhi had always led the non-cooperation campaign as if it were a calculated war, cleverly alternating attacks and retreats. This time, too, significantly, the new strategic move was to be an experiment, meant to measure the force of the *satyagrahi*, and the response of the authorities, in a territory inhabited by barely than 70,000 people.

But the Bardoli experiment was nipped in the bud. On February 4, 1922, at Chauri Chaur in the United Provinces, a crowd of parading peasants, infuriated by being taunted and then attacked by several policemen, assaulted the local police station and set it on fire. Twenty-two policemen were slaughtered. Less than a week later, against the judgment of many other nationalist leaders, Gandhi decided to terminate the non-cooperation movement. "God had warned" him for the third time, he wrote, that there was not yet in India that atmosphere of sincerity and non-violence which alone might justify mass disobedience: civil disobedience, so meek, humble, wise and astute, but loving, "never criminal nor brutal." Gandhi was arrested a month later, and con-

Arrival of the Prince of Wales on his visit to Calcutta, 1922.

demned to six years in prison (though he would be freed, in order to have an urgent operation for appendicitis, in February 1924).

The non-cooperation campaign thus terminated without bringing any immediately tangible results (another reason why some Congress politicians had opposed its early closure). But in many ways, its effects had been deep and numerous.

For the first time, a vast movement characterized by non-violent methods had embraced the cause of *swaraj*, albeit in a way that was still ambiguous. The term *swaraj* was itself ambiguous: for some, it meant inde-

pendence; for others, a beginning of self-government; for others again, the autonomy of India as a dominion, within the ambit of the British Empire. The common struggle had wrought a form of unity between Hindus and Muslims, for a relatively long period of time. Under Gandhi's guidance, Congress had consolidated its strength and transformed itself into a proper party. Gandhi's ideas and practices, from *satyagraha* to boycotts to the use of *khadi*, had been widely experimented and had become accepted by the masses. Popular mobilization had reached every corner of India, from the peaks of the Himalayas to the Dravidic regions of the south. And for the first time, the British had been clearly warned about their future presence in India.

Gandhi in 1921 during the annual session of Congress, at Ahmedabad.

In the early twenties, the population of India numbered a little over 250 million. Of these, only 200,000 were European, and among the Europeans (British in the overwhelming majority), only 70,000 had a specific function in maintaining the Empire: 60,000 in the army, 10,000 in the police or Civil Service (most of the rank-and-file soldiers, policemen, and now even administrative clerks were Indians). Among other things, Gandhi had demonstrated the impossibility of this lim-

On March 10, 1922, Gandhi was accused of sedition, and arrested. The trial was held eight days later at Ahmedabad, before District Judge Broomfield. It lasted for 100 minutes, just one hearing. Accused of trying to incite disaffection and hostility against His Majesty's Government in three articles published in his newspaper, *Young India*, Gandhi immediately pleaded guilty. When the judge asked him whether he wanted to make a declaration, he began by praising the public minister who had accused him in court: "Because the accusation is true," he said. Gandhi added that he had no desire to hide from the court the fact that "to preach disaffection toward the existing system of government has become almost a passion for me." He continued saying that he wished to avoid violence —

"Non-violence is the first article of my faith." But he had been forced to make a choice. Either he was to submit to a system that, in his opinion, had brought irreparable harm to his country, or risk seeing the mad fury of his people unleashed, after learning the truth from his lips. He recognized that at times, his people had lost control. For that reason he was present in court: not to submit to a "light penalty," but to the most severe one. He asked for no pardon, no mercy. In a spirit of joy, he was ready to submit to the heaviest penalties that could be inflicted on him, for what the law held to be a deliberate crime, but which to him, on the contrary, was "the highest duty of a citizen."
Gandhi declared that he wished to explain to the court, to the Indian public, and to the British public, too, how and

why he had gone from being a dedicated, loyal subject of British rule over India, to its implacable adversary. He talked of his political activity in South Africa, where he had discovered that "I had no rights as a man, because I was an Indian." At the time he had been fooled into thinking that the treatment reserved for Indians was "an excrescence upon a system that was intrinsically and mainly good." While criticizing its errors, therefore, he had "spontaneously and wholeheartedly" offered the government his collaboration: for example, by organizing volunteer health squads in 1899, 1906, and 1914; and again, in 1918, by attempting to recruit Indians. In all these attempts to serve the military effort, he had been sustained by the conviction that such dedication would enable him to win equal status for his compatriots within the Empire. The first shock had come with the Rowlatt Act, followed by the horror of the massacre in Punjab, the order to crawl, the custom of whipping citizens in public, and other indescribable humiliations. All his hopes had been frustrated. Reluctantly, he had come to the conclusion that the tie to England had made India even more poor and helpless than it had been previously.

Under British domination, continued Gandhi, Indian handicrafts had been "ruined by incredibly heartless and inhuman processes," and the country was no longer able to combat famine. Even the law had been used, and was still being used, to serve the interests of the rulers: his experience of political trials in India had brought him to the conclusion that in nine out of ten cases, the "condemned men were totally innocent. Their crime consisted in the love of their country... If one has no affection for a person or system," added Gandhi, "one should be free to give the fullest expression to his disaffection, so long as he does not contemplate, promote or incite to violence." But, he added, the clause by which he was accused considered any expression of disaffection to be a crime. He had studied some of the trials held on the basis of that clause: he was sure that "some of the most loved of India's patriots had been convicted under it." Gandhi went on to explain that he felt no personal malevo-

lence toward the king, nor toward single representatives of the law, but he considered it wrong to feel attachment to a system that had mortified India. He considered it a "precious privilege" to be able to write what he had written in the various articles now used as evidence against him. He was present in court, he said, in order to urge the authorities to inflict the maximum penalty that sentencing could produce for what the law considered a deliberate crime, but what to him, on the contrary, appeared to be the highest duty of a citizen. He told the judge that the only choice open to him was to resign from his post in order to disassociate himself from evil, if he felt that the law he was called on to administrate was evil, and Gandhi innocent; or else inflict on him the severest penalty, if he felt that the system he helped to administrate was right for the people, and Gandhi's activity detrimental to the country's prosperity.

Judge Broomfield seemed moved by Gandhi's words. He told Gandhi that in a way, he had made the judge's task easier by declaring himself guilty of the accusations made against him. What remained, though — the will to pronounce a just sentence — was perhaps the hardest thing a judge could find himself facing in India. The law did not consider the individual person. But it would be impossible to ignore the fact that Gandhi belonged to a completely different category from any other person that

Broomfield had ever tried, or, probably, would ever try. The judge recognized that in the eyes of millions of Gandhi's compatriots, he was a "great leader and a great patriot." Even those who did not agree with his political ideas looked to him as a man "of high ideals, and of a noble and even saintly life." But the judge was forced to consider Gandhi differently. His duty was to judge Gandhi as a citizen subject to the law. There were certainly few people in India, added the judge, who did not sincerely regret that fact that Gandhi had made it "impossible for any government to leave [him] at liberty." Broomfield suggested following a precedent from twelve years earlier, when Tilak had received a six-year prison sentence for the same crime. But, he added, if the course of events in India should make it possible for the government to reduce the sentence and free Gandhi, no one would be happier than Broomfield.

Gandhi then declared that he considered it a great privilege and honor to be associated with the name of Tilak. In recognition of the courtesy with which the whole trial had proceeded, he continued to smile calmly as his friends crowded around him in tears to say good-bye. He was then taken outside the courtroom and led back to prison, only to be transferred, two days later, to the central prison of Yeravda, near Pune. Here he would actually remain for a shorter time than expected, about twenty-three months. ∎

ited minority continuing to govern India for long without the consensus and collaboration of the Indians themselves. Nevertheless, the British would resist heeding this lesson for a long time to come.

Years of Waiting

After leaving the Yeravda prison, Gandhi found himself facing a changed and painful situation. India was beset by conflict and violence. First of all, the Hindu-Muslim hostilities had flared up again. The era of collaboration between the two communities now seemed distant, and violent attacks between them had once again become everyday affairs. In September 1924, Gandhi began a twenty-one day fast, in the home of his Muslim friend, Mohammed Ali, in order to expiate, and to persuade Hindus and Muslims to do penance. This initiative, however, obtained only modest results, though it did help to attract attention to the seriousness of the Hindu-Muslim problem.

Conflict prevailed in Congress, as well. It was divided between *swarajists*, such as Das and Motilal Nehru, who advocated participation in the electoral process (though with the intention of carrying on the anti-British struggle from within); and the so-called "no-changers," such as Patel and the younger Nehru, who had remained faithful to Gandhi's policy of non-cooperation.

GANDHI'S FASTS

Gandhi's great fasts numbered seventeen. The first ones, lasting respectively for one and two weeks, were carried out in South Africa in 1913 and 1914: Gandhi undertook them as acts of reparation for the grave errors committed by members of his community. Later on, in India, Gandhi fasted in order to support workers' rights; to protest against British political decisions that he believed to be unacceptable, or against injustice of which he was victim; to expiate acts of intolerance and violence on the part of his followers in the anti-British struggle. His last two fasts were particularly dramatic. They took place in Calcutta in 1947, and in Delhi in 1948, a few days before he was assassinated, and they were meant to put a stop to the Hindu-Muslim conflict. Of these seventeen fasts, five were carried out while Gandhi was in prison (four of them, in 1932-1933, in the Yeravda prison). The three longest fasts lasted for twenty-one days. In at least two cases, in 1933 and 1948, the prolonged abstinence from food gravely endangered the Mahatma's life. The total duration of the seventeen fasts was 151 days: but this figure obviously does not include his many other, more "private" fasts, undertaken for the sake of purification and to strengthen his powers of spiritual concentration (Gandhi was a confirmed believer in the bond between diet, control of the body, and control of the spirit). ■

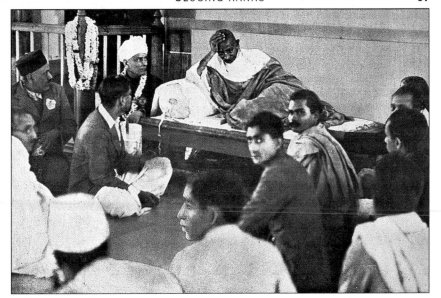

Gandhi was forced to accept Congress's approval of the *swarajists'* position, but during the year 1925, he virtually abandoned active politics, in order to dedicate himself to the social problems of India.

Gandhi in meditation, surrounded by a group of followers.

He resumed his journeys throughout India, supported the untouchables' cause, publicized the use of *khadi* and founded a pan-Indian spinners' association; he tried to stimulate educational experiences and to spread compliance with norms of health and cleanliness in the villages; he fought alcoholism, organized campaigns against premature marriage, advocated women's rights in society and in the family (Gandhi called women "the better half of heaven"). Little by little, during the years that followed, he grouped all these objectives together in a general project destined to be approved by Congress. At the basis of this program was the idea that fighting for independence presupposes a profound cultural and social reform, starting from the masses of the Indian populace.

He also dedicated himself to the material and spiritual consolidation of his *ashram*, which now welcomed new followers and received continuous visits from admirers and the curious, Indians and Europeans alike. The newcomers included a young lady from England,

Madeleine Slade: she had heard of Gandhi from her
father, an admiral who had resided in India, and decided to join him. With the Indian name given her by
the Mahatma, Mirabehn, she would remain at his side,
a precious collaborator, right up to the end.

Gandhi decided to spend the entire year of 1926 in
meditation, and in a seldom-interrupted silence; and
from that year on, he would spend one day a week —
Monday — in total silence. In 1924 he also began to
write and publish in serial form his autobiography, which
he would finish five years later. He entitled it *Autobiography, or My Experiments with Truth.*

In the meantime, between 1924 and 1928, the political situation in the country was becoming ever more
tense and complex. The British had forcefully taken control again after the great non-cooperation campaign of

1920–1922. However, India was being
swept by new and ancient conflicts: religious, tribal, and social. In 1924, an Indian Communist Party was born. One of
its young advocates, Menabendra Nath
Roy, enjoyed great prestige within the
Third International, where he made a
name for himself in debates on the revolution in Asia. Within India, the Communist Party would always play a limited and
minor role. Still, it did contribute to the
spread of Marxism, revolutionary ideas,
and sympathy for the Soviet Union: Jawaharlal Nehru himself was influenced by it.
Communist groups participated in the formation of labor unions, which led a series of workers' battles. There were
demonstrations on the part of laborers
and farmers, and even a relaunching of
terrorism.

*Above, Gandhi and Jawaharlal
Nehru, 1935.*

This increase in tension echoed throughout the political world: both by influencing it directly, and thus
radicalizing the positions of young leaders like Jawaharlal Nehru and Subhas Chandra Bose; and by making the old leaders fearful of being overtaken by mass
movements that risked spinning out of control.

In 1928 a commission arrived in India which was

Gandhi was acquainted with *Das Capital*, and several other works by Marx and Engels, as well as works by Lenin and Stalin, and writings on Chinese Communism. His analysis of the Soviet revolution, for which he nurtured a kind of respect, nevertheless helped to further convince him of the dangers of using violence for revolutionary ends. He was worried by the costs of violent social revolutions, by the prospect that one day the poor might become just as "bad" as their present masters and exploiters. Finding himself, if anything, more in sympathy with the anarchist tradition, he held — as did Thoreau — that the best government is the one that governs least. When talking with Louis Fischer in 1946, Gandhi described the differences between his own "socialism" and Russian Socialism: his, in its modified form, meant that the State owned nothing. In Russia, on the contrary, the State was owner, and so a person could not be the master even "of his own body." You could be arrested "at any time, without having committed any crime." And they could send you anywhere they wanted. "I," declared Gandhi, "desire a free world. This is not the wish of the Communists. They want a system that reduces the spirit to slavery."

Many years before, in 1924, he had written that he did not yet know exactly what Bolshevism was, not having had the chance to study it. He did not know whether in the long term it would bring good to Russia. But he was sure that, to the extent that it was based on violence and on "the negation of God," he could not accept it. He refused to believe in victories obtained in the haste of violence. And in 1928, in an article rendering honor to the "purest sacrifice of innumerable men and women" which had been made during the Bolshevik experiment, and to "an ideal consecrated by the sacrifices" of men of the moral level of Lenin, he insisted that the use of force in the expropriation of private property and in the maintenance of collective state property would bring Bolshevism to an early end: "nothing lasting can be built on violence." In another article, in 1925, he expressed his view that the heroism and sacrifice spent by revolutionaries for an unjust cause were "an enormous waste of splendid energies." Romain Rolland was a typical representative of the leftist European intelligentsia in the thirties, who considered the USSR to be the "hope of the world." When Gandhi went to visit him in 1931, Rolland tried in every way to convert him to his theories, even praising the exercise of justice in the Soviet Union. But Gandhi put up a strenuous resistance. Force was the "basis" of Soviet methods, he said. The Indians who were under the influence of Russian methods had assumed positions of great intolerance, and the practice of terrorism. ■

named after Sir John Simon, the liberal British politician presiding over it. The commission had been assigned the task of studying the future constitutional development of the country, but since it was composed only of Englishmen, the Indians boycotted it. Its arrival resulted mainly in a harrowing series of strikes, protest demonstrations, and terrorist attacks. As a response, the government intervened harshly with police and military action in a number of localities. Because of blows inflicted on him by the *lathi* (the long nightsticks used by the police), Lala Lajpat Raj, one of the most prestigious heads of Congress, died. In 1929, thirty-one union leaders were arrested and accused of conspiracy. Nehru was the principle lawyer for their defense in a famous trial in Meerut which lasted four years and finally resulted in harsh sentences for all.

The salt march, after leaving Sabarmati on March 12, 1929.

The Salt March

In the story of India's struggle for independence, the last days of 1929 and the first of 1930 represent a dramatic turning point. The preceding months had seen the last remaining hopes of the Indian nationalists gradually crumble: the hope, that is, that the British authorities would grant dominion status to India. The Congress that met in Lahore in December of 1929 could do nothing beyond recognizing the reality of the situation. The more moderate traditional leaders were deprived of political force. For the first time, and with Gandhi's support, young Jawaharlal Nehru was elected president. Congress approved a document declaring an all-out movement for complete independence (*purna swaraj*), and announced a new campaign of civil disobedience. Gandhi carried the effort forward on January 31, 1930, by presenting in his newspaper, *Young India*, a list of claims gathered under the heading

"Eleven Points." These were meant to bring together the greatest number of social groups possible. His demands ranged from reduction of the land tax to the reduction of military expenses, from abolition of the salt tax to the liberation of political prisoners, to the imposition of import duties on foreign fabrics. But during those months, Gandhi was involved above all in seeking out the fairest and most effective way to relaunch civil disobedience. He thought it over furiously, as he told Tagore, day and night. Eventually he zeroed in on his objective: to regain for Indians the right to mine salt, and thus break the government monopoly. Many of the Mahatma's companions in the struggle reacted to this idea with mistrust and concern. The objective seemed too limited to them, hardly capable of involving large masses of Indians — from a material point of view, only the poorest fringes of the coastal populace could ever join in such a campaign. But Gandhi had acutely perceived its symbolic significance.

*O*n March 5, 1930 the British authorities arrest Gandhi. This is how the episode was illustrated in Italy, by Achille Beltrame, for readers of the Domenica del Corriere.

On March 12, Gandhi left his *ashram* in Sabarmati, in the company of seventy-eight other *satyagrahi*, and headed for the coastal town of Dandi, 230 miles away. The youngest participant in the "salt march" was sixteen years of age; the oldest was Gandhi himself, then sixty-one. Great crowds gathered along the way, or accompanied the group for short distances. They reached Dandi on April 6. Gandhi walked into the sea and pulled out a handful of salt.

At first the British authorities had chosen to remain on the sidelines, counting on the probability that the initiative would fail. But when millions of Indians throughout the land

began to imitate the Mahatma by gathering salt and handing it out, while boycotting British products or resigning from government posts, then the repression began. Between March and May, from 60,000 to 90,000 Indians were arrested, while at least a hundred were

killed by police, and thousands wounded. Those arrested included Nehru; the two Patels; Rajagopalachari; Mohan Madan Malaviya; Gandhi's secretary, Mahadev Desai, and one of the Mahatma's sons, Devadas. Finally, on May 5, Gandhi himself was imprisoned.

The viceroy, Lord Irwin (later Lord Halifax) was not, however, an advocate of purely repressive methods. He tried to approach the most influential men of Congress (nearly all of whom were in jail) in order to discuss the possibility that one or more of their representatives might participate in the first Round Table Conference on the future of India, planned for that year in London. But his invitations came to nothing, and the Conference opened and closed amidst general indifference. The historian, Wolpert, wrote that with no representation from Congress, it was like performing *Hamlet* without the Prince of Denmark.

The year 1931 opened dramatically. On January 25, Lord Irwin freed Gandhi and the members of the Executive Committee of Congress. This gesture of reconciliation had been opposed by most of the viceroy's advisers: these included Indian notables who collaborated with the British administration, some of the Muslims, and above all, the heads of bureaucracy, the army, and the police. But Lord Irwin intended to resume a dialogue, and Gandhi's response was positive.

Between February 17 and March 4, Gandhi had eight encounters with Lord Irwin. Their eventual outcome was the so-called Delhi Pact, or Gandhi-Irwin Pact. It provided for the cessation of civil disobedience, in exchange for the liberation of political prisoners arrested for committing acts connected with it (no liberation was foreseen for those who had been arrested and tried for acts of violence). The pact allowed the inhabitants of coastal areas to mine small quantities of salt, and recognized the right to boycott foreign fabrics, but it did not grant restitution for employment lost as a consequence of the civil disobedience campaign. It made no mention of a demand that was dear to the nationalists: an inquiry into police excesses during the repression. It recognized that defense, foreign policy, minority problems, and finances should fall into Britain's area of competence, "in the interest of India." Nehru and other leaders were upset by these concessions, which represented a big step backward with respect to the deliberations of the Lahore Congress, and to Gandhi's Eleven Points. But Gandhi held that the moment always arrives when a *satyagrahi* whose aim is always to "convert the adversary with love," cannot refuse to deal with the opposition.

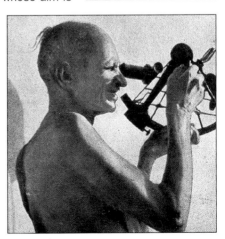

On the Rajputana, *the steamship carrying him to Europe, Gandhi amuses himself by using navigating instruments.*

Application of the pact was difficult for both sides. Tension and upheaval occurred in Bengal and Bombay. With tireless effort, Gandhi reached another agreement with the new viceroy, Lord Willingdon, who was more implacable and less conciliatory than his predecessor. In the meantime Congress decided to send Gandhi to London, as its single representative at the Round Table.

In Europe

On August 29, Gandhi set sail for Bombay on the steamship *Rajputana*. He was accompanied by his son, Devadas, his two secretaries (Mahadev Desai and the younger Pyarelal), and the faithful Mirabehn (Miss

Slade). Others of Gandhi's followers were traveling on the same ship: the woman poet, Sarojini Naidu, Mohan Madan Malaviya, and G.D. Birla. The latter, invited to the Conference as a representative of the business world, was an entrepreneur tied to Gandhi by deep bonds of friendship. He was also a financial supporter of Gandhi's movement, which was ever in dire need of economic assistance. ("The Mahatma," joked Sarojini Naidu once, "hasn't got the slightest idea how much his poverty costs us.")

On board the *Rajputana* Gandhi was traveling second class (there was no third class). He was amused and intrigued by everything, like a boy on vacation. His secretary, Mahadev Desai, observed that he spent most of the day and the whole night on deck. He got up and went to bed at the usual hours, and followed the same routine of prayer, spinning, and study that he had followed at the *ashram.* The children of the English passengers returning to their homeland became his friends; they watched him use the spinning wheel, and when they peered in at his cabin in the morning or evening, they were given bunches of grapes and dates.

Londoners welcome Gandhi upon his arrival for the Round Table Conference, September 1931.

While chatting with Birla on board ship, he confided his desire to meet the eminent Winston Churchill, precisely because he opposed the Indian cause; whereas he was considerably less interested in meeting people like George Bernard Shaw. Shortly before, Churchill had declared that he found photographs of that "semi-naked fakir" who treated the viceroy and the king as equals, to be "nauseating."

Gandhi arrived in London on September 12, and went to stay in the home of a philanthropist who assisted the destitute of Bow, a working-class neighborhood in

the East End; she had gone to visit him in 1926. He was very happy with this arrangement, which allowed him to stay "among the same class of people to whom he had dedicated his life." The second Round Table Conference began a few days later, and ended at the beginning of December.

It was a miserable failure. Gandhi had nurtured the illusion that he could represent and symbolize the unity of the nationalist movement in India. With great frankness, he asked that India and England be permitted to create an honorable association, based on parity. But in London, there was no unity in the Indian nationalist movement. Yes, Gandhi did represent the organization which was most numerous and militant, by far; but he was also one among many delegates to the Conference, which include maharajas, representatives of the Muslim minority, the untouchables, Indian Christians, and the business world. On more than one occasion, the gathering of delegates offered a depressing spectacle of division and bickering. The respect which generally surrounded the figure of Gandhi did not prevent this divisiveness, and the British were quick to play upon it. They applied the old strategy of divide and conquer and justified it by pleading the necessity of taking into account the rights of all interested communities. Moreover, they were able to bring the discussion down from a level of principle, most favored by Gandhi, to a level of minor problems, such as that of local autonomies. While the Conference was being held there was a crisis in government, and in the new coalition the conservatives increased their power. This

A meeting of the Round Table Conference. The photos taken on this occasion usually show a Gandhi disappointed and irritated by the way the proceedings were going.

change contributed heavily to strengthening the position of those who believed that the loss of India would
permanently weaken the British Empire. The Conference thus crawled listlessly along without any results,
except to delegate the Indian problem to future com-
missions charged with inquiring into it.

Gandhi was deeply disappointed by this outcome. He
was slightly less disappointed regarding a different goal
he had set. "Here I am," he had said shortly after his
arrival in London, "ready to take on the real work of
the round table, by getting acquainted with the English."
During a month and a half, Gandhi spoke with hundreds
of people from every walk of life, and shook thousands
of hands. He was received in Court by George V. He
met members of Parliament,
bishops, university profes-
sors, and students. He did not
meet Churchill, but did have
occasion to chat with Shaw,
who considered himself a "minor Mahatma." He received a
visit from Charlie Chaplin,
whom he had never heard of,
but whom he gladly agreed to
meet once he heard that Chaplin, too, came from a poor family (Chaplin had grown up in the
East End). Gandhi spoke to
Chaplin of his aversion to the
machine civilization — his conviction that it renders man a
slave. On the contrary, Chaplin
— who five years later would
direct *Modern Times* — de-
fended the advantages of modern science and technology.

Disappointment with the Round Table proceedings was counterbalanced by the great popular success that Gandhi enjoyed in England. Here he is surrounded by a crowd of women in Lancashire.

Above all, as he tirelessly made the rounds of the
poorest neighborhoods of London, Gandhi became a
favorite of the common people, especially of children.
"Thousands and thousands of children in England,"
wrote his secretary, Desai, "will have seen Gandhi before he leaves the shores of England." And, he added,
perhaps it would be this next generation with which

the Mahatma, and India, would really have to come to terms.

Gandhi also visited Lancashire, in order to speak with those workers in the cotton industry who, more than anyone else, had been harmed by the boycott declared by Congress against English fabrics. He explained to them that if it was true that their salaries were very low, his compatriots' conditions were incomparably worse; he was applauded and feted on this occasion too. A short time later, he wrote that during his stay in East London, he had seen the best side of human nature, and had been confirmed in his intuitive opinion that, after all, East and West do not exist. The experience had drawn him even closer to England, assuming that such was possible.

*G*andhi with Charlie Chaplin, at their London meeting in 1931. On the Mahatma's left (right for the reader) is the poet Sarojini Naidu.

Gandhi left London on December 5. He made his first stopover in Paris, where he spoke in a cinema, before a great crowd. He left the next morning for Villeneuve, in Switzerland, where Romain Rolland was awaiting him. Rolland was perhaps the most influential member of a sort of "international" composed of Gandhi's admirers, scattered all over Europe. Rolland had been almost unrivalled in spreading the Europeans' knowledge of Gandhi: he had published collections of the Mahatma's writings, as well as his biography. For several days, Gandhi spent long hours talking with Rolland, and also spoke to many attentive audiences in Geneva and Lausanne. On December 11 he left for Milan, and then for Rome, where he was received by Mussolini for a brief talk. On the morning of December 14 he set sail from Brindisi for Bombay.

While Gandhi was in Europe, his disappointment at the way the Conference had gone was aggravated by the worrying news coming out of India. Bengal, the United Provinces, and the northwest frontier continued to be areas of upheaval. Disappointment at the failure of the Conference, and at Britain's failure to comply with

GANDHI IN FASCIST ITALY

In December of 1931, in the course of his return journey from London back to India, Gandhi stopped in Italy for three days. After a brief stopover in Milan he arrived in Rome, where he remained nearly all the time he was in Italy. Then he left for Brindisi, where he boarded the steamship that would take him back to India.

It was Gino Scarpa, the Italian Consul in Calcutta, who had first invited Gandhi to Italy; however, both the diplomatic sector and the Italian political world disagreed over the wisdom of this invitation. The Anglophiles among government figures worried about upsetting the British government by offering hospitality to its rival. On the other hand, the more anti-British ones (probably including Mussolini himself) were inclined to make contact with him, with an eye to future opportunities for Italian policy in Asia. At any rate, measures were taken to limit the impact and official formalities of his visit. Gandhi was taken around to visit schools, youth centers and other institutions of the regime. He was nearly always welcomed by Fascist leaders in uniform, and by squads of armed vanguard soldiers. He was not received by the foreign minister, but did talk with the Duce for ten minutes. According to accounts given by witnesses, it was a cordial, but politically insignificant chat,

and it was nearly always Mussolini who did the talking. Gandhi had accepted the invitation because he never wanted to lose an opportunity to publicize the Indian cause, and also because he had hoped to meet the Pope, Pius XI, and speak with him about the Indian Catholics. For these reasons he had resisted pressure from people like Rolland and the anti-Fascist exiles who tried to persuade him not to travel to Italy or to meet with the Fascist dictator. As it turned out, the Pope did not receive him, and Gandhi had very few occasions in Rome to discuss the problems of his people, or to illustrate his theory of non-violence. As consolation, he was treated warmly (and not only with curiosity) by numerous people on the streets of the capital; he was moved at the sight of the Sistine Chapel and the Vatican Museums; and he received a visit from Tatyana Tolstoy, daughter of the great Russian writer whom he so greatly admired. But all in all, his trip to Italy was rather disappointing. At any rate, Gandhi, his thought, and his works were fairly well-known in Italy at the time. Italian editors had already published biographies of him (including the most famous one, written by Rolland) and collected many of his writings, together with numerous articles by newspaper reporters writing about him from India. In that same year of 1931 a translation of his autobiography had come out, with an introduction by Giovanni Gentile. There were several attempts to involve Gandhi in the Fascist movement by depicting his thought and activities as harmonious with Fascism (although such a process involved a considerable effort of the imagination). But above all, there were anti-Fascist Italian "Gandhians" — though few in number. The most famous of them, Aldo Capitini, was to remember thereafter the importance of his encounter with the thought and example of Gandhi. ∎

the Gandhi-Irwin Pact had increased tensions, riots, and acts of terrorism. The situation was worsened by the government's attitude. The new viceroy, Lord Willingdon, ordered a vast series of repressive measures, along with the arrest of many nationalist leaders. When Gandhi stepped on shore at Bombay on December 28, he found there an inflamed and increasingly uncontrollable situation. One week later he was arrested, for the fourth time in his life. This time he was locked up in the Yeravda prison and would remain there for fifteen months.

The Untouchables

After being released in August of 1933, Gandhi did not return to prison again for nearly nine years. At any rate, he had always shown great serenity in facing what he jokingly dubbed the king and emperor's hospitality. He liked to say that it had given him the opportunity to devote himself to his studies. As we learn from his diaries, he actually did take advantage of his numerous stays in jail in order to read. He read a great deal, and he read everything: Indian and Western works, religious writings, political and historical essays, and fiction, too.

After 1933 Gandhi became less active in the field of politics, choosing to dedicate himself, instead, to a "constructive program" and to the internal problems of India. For a time he had hoped that independence was near, but now he saw how slow and weak were the reforms being proposed. Furthermore, he now realized how oppressed Indians were by ancient rivalries and customs. Once more he chose to travel, and talk to the people. He preached *satyagraha*, explaining that it was not intended to function only as a strategy of conflict, but as a means of spiritual renewal for all Indians, making them worthy of independence and capable of administrating it, once they had attained it. He was very cautious when dealing with the problem of castes, but did not hesitate to support the rights of untouchables, whom he called *harijan*, "children of God."

Gandhi had always opposed the idea of separate electorates for Hindus and Muslims, because he dreamed of an India where everyone could live together in peace as members of a single nation, not segregated

"The golden rule of conduct is mutual tolerance, since we shall never all have the same ideas, and we shall never see the Truth except in a fragmentary way, from different angles of vision."

On the left, Gandhi in Italy with children from a Fascist youth organization.
© Publifoto

by religion. He expressed a similar attitude regarding the untouchables, opposing the creation of separate polls for them. Such separation was supported by a great leader of the outcasts, B.R. Ambedkar, a jurist who, several years later, would head the commission in charge of writing the constitution of independent India. Ambedkar held that the outcasts, "treated like lepers," were too weak within Indian society to be able to compete on an equal level; therefore, they should be protected and defended by special measures. Gandhi considered this position to be an obstacle to his goal of purifying Hinduism of its most terrible stain.

The question had already come up in 1932, when the British government announced election reforms creating separate polling stations for the minorities: not only for the Muslims (who already had them), but also for Sikhs, Indian Christians, Anglo-Indians, Europeans, and the "deprived classes." Gandhi, who was then in Yeravda prison, immediately began a fast "unto death;" as a man of religion, he said, he had no other choice. Ambedkar, who had previously criticized Gandhi's position, met with him at Yeravda and reached an accord with him after a week of difficult negotiations. The agreement (which was then accepted by the viceroy) declared that, in principle, there would be no separate polling stations; the untouchables would participate in the elections as normal voters. However, they would in reality be guaranteed more seats than had previously been foreseen.

Gandhi persuaded authorized representatives of the high castes to come to Yeravda in order to sign the pact reached with Ambedkar. In the days immediately following, he demanded that his followers open thousands of temples to the *harijan*. He also founded a society for the assistance of untouchables, and a weekly newspaper, *Harijan*, printed both in English and in Hindi, to which he would entrust many of his next writ-

Calcutta, 1934, students offer Gandhi donations for the harijan movement.

ings. Therefore, the "Yeravda Pact" (accompanied by the suspension of Gandhi's fast) came to be understood as a clear denunciation of untouchability, the beginning of its end. It declared that no person was to be considered untouchable by birth, and that untouchables could not be denied use of public wells, schools, or streets. In much of India people celebrated a "week for the abolition of untouchability," though the formal abolition of untouchable status would not be proclaimed until after attaining independence. And since customs and traditions have roots too deep to be destroyed by a simple legislative act, the inferior condition of the outcasts would persist for a long time to come (it still does today, in many ways). However the "Yeravda Pact" was a decisive step forward along the road to emancipation.

In 1933, Gandhi abandoned his *satyagraha ashram* at Sabarmati, and three years later, moved to the village of Segaon, near Wardha, in the heart of India. He named his new headquarters *Sevagram*, or "village of service": more than an ashram, he forged it into a model village community, organized according to the criteria of his "constructive program."

Entrance to the central prison at Yeravda, near Pune. All together, Gandhi spent three and a half years there, where he wrote some of his works. When asked once to give his address, he jokingly answered, "Yeravda Prison."

GANDHI IN PRISON

Gandhi first became acquainted with His Majesty's prisons on January 10, 1908, in Johannesburg, and was released from his last period of detention on May 6, 1944 (in Bombay, where he had been imprisoned for twenty-one months in the Aga Khan's villa, like other leaders of the Congress Party, during World War II). He was arrested twelve times, and spent slightly more than five years of his life in jail. It would have been for twice that number of years, if the British had always made him serve his entire sentences. ∎

A demonstration in favor of swadeshi *in Karachi. The demonstrators gather foreign goods onto the back of a donkey and parade them around, before burning them in a bonfire.*
© Publifoto

In the thirties, again, Gandhi intensified his national campaign in favor of *khadi*. With this move, among other things, he intended to remind Indians that their textile handicrafts had been destroyed by the competition of British products, and persuade them to boycott those products. But *swadeshi*, the love and preservation of traditional things like hand spinning, was not only an economic strategy. *Swadeshi*, said Gandhi, is the tendency in our spirit which leads us to use things that are nearby, in preference over those that are far away. As we have seen, Gandhi did not love big industry, or anything that destroys nature, or separates human beings from it. Living in a poor, overpopulated country, he had no great hopes for a European type of economic development in the (distant) future, but preferred to enliven the villages by stimulating the initiative and energy of the peasant masses who lived there.

Hindus and Muslims: On the Eve of Conflict

In 1935, a new Government of India Act was promulgated: the last of India's constitutions to be conceived and determined exclusively by the British. It widened the autonomy of the provinces, making its ministers responsible to elective assemblies except in the fields of defense and finance. (However, it still gave the provincial governor wide powers of control and intervention.) It extended suffrage greatly, but still preserved certain limitations connected with census standing. The number of Indian voters grew from 6.5 million to about thirty-five million, including six million women; and more than three million untouchables. The new constitution also made provision for the formation of a federation among the provinces and the princely states, but this federation remained only on paper.

Congress assumed a critical attitude, both because of the limited nature of powers granted to the Indians, and because it could not agree to letting the more than 500 maharajas — this relic of the past! — govern on the same level as the provinces. However, it decided to participate all the same in the elections of 1937–1938 and, to the bewilderment of the British even more than the Indians, it won, polling 70 percent of the popular vote. Besides the prestige of Gandhi and other leaders, what contributed to Congress's success was its almost complete transformation into a modern political party, with roots sinking into all of India and into every social class. Another contributing factor was the entrance into the party's ranks of numerous local notables, even if they were often motivated less by nationalist passion than by the desire to feel protected by a strong organization. Members of Congress were able to form local governments in seven provinces.

On the other hand, the Muslim League had a poor showing at the polls, obtaining less than a quarter of the seats reserved to Muslims in India. But in the provinces where Muslims were in the majority, Congress had not been victorious in the elections, either. There, the voters mostly had chosen regional groups and parties.

With Muhammad Ali Jinnah, leader of the Muslim League; in the decisive years of the struggle for independence, he would become Gandhi's implacable rival.

The Muslim League had gone into a steady decline, tiredly dragging along in an apathy that had been interrupted only for a moment in 1930. That year a poet from Punjab, Muhammad Iqbal, had inflamed a political session by proposing the creation of a majority Muslim state in the northwest of India; soon afterwards, some young Muslims studying at Cambridge had suggested a name for that state. It would be called Pakistan, meaning "Land of the Pure" and also an acronym formed by the initials of several provinces with a Muslim majority (Punjab, Afghan Provinces, Kashmir, and Sindh) plus the final letters of Baluchistan. Immediately afterwards, apathy returned. But in 1935, after years of absence from politics (and from India itself), Muhammad Ali Jinnah had decided to take up leadership of the League: too late to obtain satisfying results as early as 1937–1938, but in time to set the League on the road to becoming a great party as well. Jinnah was able to exploit the fears

The Mahatma with Subhas Chandra Bose in 1938.

of many Muslims that once independence had been won, they would find themselves overrun by a Hindu majority. The economic and social conflicts that had often threatened peaceful coexistence between the two communities did the rest. Quite soon, strengthened under the guidance of Jinnah, the League demanded that the British consider it the only representative of the fragmented world of Indian Islam. Gandhi and Congress could not accept this ambitious claim, because they had always aimed at representing the nationalist movement of the entire Indian populace, above and beyond religious differences: many Muslims, after all, were leaders or followers of Congress, even though its leadership was mostly Hindu. Some, such as Nehru, strongly feared the future "Balkanization" of the country, should other ethnic, linguistic, or religious communities start to make secessionist claims. The unity of India was something Congress would never renounce. This radical conflict of opinion revealed its seriousness and danger as early as 1938, with the failure of talks between the two political forces.

But the Hindu-Muslim conflict was not the only problem darkening the horizon that year. When put to the test, the provincial governing forces of Congress found themselves facing uncontrollable social schisms, aggravated by the fact that peasants and workers, entrepreneurs and big landowners were all competing within the party itself. People very suddenly passed from a level of great ideals to the work of daily negotiation, and sometimes, to corruption.

The mystique of Gandhi, who had been away from the political scene for several years, was criticized or openly challenged by new, more radical leaders: in particular by Subhas Chandra Bose, who was elected president of Congress in 1938. However, in the months that followed, Bose was unable to stave off the hostility of Gandhi's faithful, and so he ended up leaving the presidency, and Congress itself.

Finally, the entire country and especially the leaders sensitive to the problem of democracy, were oppressed by the darkening clouds of imminent war: a war threatening freedom, and threatening to involve Asia directly. This danger led the British, in particular, to become more and more rigid in their positions: they feared that they would no longer be able to count on India as their most solid pillar in defense of their empire. In reality, the war would hasten the end of the British Empire and the achievement of Indian independence, but at the price of a historic tragedy destined to betray and, to a great extent, thwart the mostly non-violent nature of the Indian nationalist movement.

War

On September 3, 1939, the viceroy decided that India would enter the war. He neglected to consult any Indian political representative. Many leaders of Congress were worried about the possibility of Britain's defeat at the hands of the Axis powers; but, as Nehru said, being against Hitler and Mussolini did not mean forgetting one's primary task: to liberate India.

In any case, the fact that suddenly, India had found itself involved in war without even being previously informed (as had also happened during the First World War) could only be interpreted as an abuse, an offense to the nation. In the view of the Indian leaders, the gravest offense was that the British had not clarified the objectives of the war, particularly in terms of the future of India. As for Gandhi, he immediately ex-

"For me patriotism is the same as humanity ... My patriotism is not exclusive: it is calculated not only not to hurt any other nation, but to benefit all in the true sense of the word. India's freedom as conceived by me can never be a menace to the world."

—Young India, *April 1924.*

pressed his moral objection to the war in the name of non-violence. He wrote an appeal to the British; he even wrote two letters to Hitler (though they were blocked by the government) to convince him of the superiority

of non-violence. Later, when the Japanese and their Indian ally, Bose, went so far as to threaten the northeastern border of India, Gandhi seems to have declared that where the British army was involved in combat with the "enemy," it was inadvisable to employ non-violent resistance. Non-violent resistance, in fact, does not proceed parallel to, nor "ally itself to violence."

Members of the Indian community in France during a reception in their honor, in London, 1940.
© Publifoto

And in 1943, he is said to have reacted harshly while speaking to an interviewer, to Britain's accusation that he was in fact on the side of the Axis. "I have called the Fascists and the Nazis," he said, "the scum of the earth."

But in 1939, Gandhi launched a campaign of non-violent opposition, though its scope was limited at first. A friend and follower of his, Vinoba Bhave, and Nehru himself, were the first to let themselves be imprisoned. They were soon followed by thousands of other *satyagrahi*. All the ministers of Congress resigned from their posts in provincial governments, to the joy of Jinnah and the Muslim League, who saw new strategic opportunities open up for them now that the field had been swept clear of rivals.

In the months that followed, Congress indeed found itself fighting a harsh battle on two fronts: against the British and against the Muslim League. In 1940, Jinnah had led a Muslim League assembly in Lahore to adopt a resolution favoring separation, and the formation of Pakistan (though that name was not explicitly used). Gandhi called the resolution an invitation to the "vivisection" of India. Ministers of the League entered some of the provincial governments abandoned by members of Congress, while the British looked benevolently on the prudence and moderation shown them by Jinnah. The head of the League insisted on the idea of his own exclusive representation of Indian Islam, and supported the theory of "two nations," a Hindu one and a Muslim one, which were historically and culturally different. For its part, Congress reaffirmed its own right to represent all Indians. To confirm this right, it elected a Muslim, Maulana Azad, to its presidency; he would remain in that post throughout the war.

The Japanese victories in Southeast Asia worried the British, and led even the proudest adversary of Indian nationalism, Winston Churchill, to accept negotiations (though quite unwillingly). In 1942, a mission arrived in India guided by a Labour Party minister in the coalition government, Sir Stafford Cripps. He brought with him a proposal which was intended as a concession to the Indian nationalists who were capable of easing tensions in the country. At the end of the war, a self-governing Indian Union was to be formed, which each

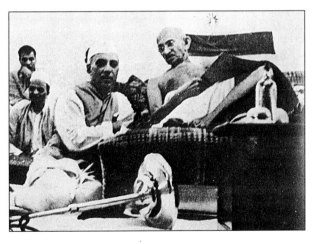

Gandhi and Nehru during a session of Congress, 1942.

state or province could freely join. In reality, this proposal left the way open to all sorts of secessionist movements, beginning with the one involving Pakistan. Besides, it did nothing to modify the existing situation during the war. The Stafford Cripps mission ended in failure. Congress rejected it harshly and implacably, and immediately afterwards relaunched the anti-British campaign, with a new slogan: *Quit India!* Mass demonstrations broke out nearly everywhere, and in some provinces there were actual riots. Groups of young people assaulted police stations and sabotaged railways and telegraph lines. The repressive response was extremely harsh: by the

Soldiers of Bose's Indian National Army, allied with the Japanese, in 1944 near Kohima, where the British stopped Japan's last attack against India. As we can see, traditional weapons are used side by side with modern weapons provided by the Japanese. The real nature of the INA's contribution to the war operation is still an actively debated question among scholars.

end of 1943, it was estimated that there had been 91,836 arrests, and that 1,060 demonstrators and sixty-three police had died in the upheaval.

On August 9, 1942, as all the other leaders of Congress already had been, Gandhi was arrested. He was imprisoned for nearly two years in the palace of the Aga Khan at Pune. It was there that, his faithful secretary, Mahadev Desai, and then his wife, Kasturbai, died beside him. Kasturbai had been near him through numberless battles, for more than sixty years. "We were," wrote Gandhi in response to the viceroy's condolence message, "an uncommon couple."

Jinnah had deplored the "open rebellion" of Congress, and kept to his moderate position. When Gandhi was freed from prison in 1944, the two had various talks which remained fruitless. Fruitless, too, were the negotiations begun by the British at the Simla Conference immediately after the end of the war. The fracture between the League and Congress now seemed irreparable.

Independence and the Death of Gandhi

World War II had created in India, too, an irreparable situation. More than two million soldiers from the Indian army, most of whom were now being demobilized, had fought at various battlefronts, especially in Africa and the Middle East, although with fewer casualties than during World War I. It was unthinkable that their participation in the military effort was not to be in any way recognized or rewarded. An acute sign of the malaise that marked the post-war period was the mutiny of squadrons of the airforce and navy. And inside the country, while the war years had seen the growth of the nationalist movement, the imprisonment of its leaders had made them assume the role of heroes, even more dramatically than before.

One episode that gave the British considerable food for thought was the trial of the soldiers who had followed Bose. It was held in Delhi in the winter of 1945–1946. After leaving the Congress Party, in 1939 Bose had formed an extremist movement in Bengal called the Forward Block Party. He was arrested but managed to escape, first reaching Moscow and then Germany by exploiting the situation created by the German-Soviet pact. He had always nurtured sympathy for Hitler and Mussolini, taking for himself the name *Netaji* ("Guide," "Leader," like the Duce and the Führer). After a daringly adventurous submarine voyage from Hamburg to Singapore in 1943, Bose had organized an army of Indian ex-prisoners of war: the INA or Indian National Army. This he had managed to accomplish with the help of the Japanese. Alongside the Japanese he had attacked Burma and northeast India. But the Anglo-Indian troops had resisted, and in 1945 Bose's army had surrendered at Rangoon (he himself died at Formosa shortly afterwards, in a mysterious airplane crash).

*F*ighting between Hindus and Muslims in Calcutta, 1946.
© Publifoto

At the trial, his ex-soldiers were defended by lawyers Nehru and Jinnah, among others. They received sentences of varying harshness, and all were released on probation. This trial rebounded against the British. Most Indians openly sided with the accused: the era of pro-British loyalty had evidently ended; now they felt a proud solidarity with those who had taken up arms against the British colonialists.

In fact, at the end of World War II, the theme of decolonization demanded attention in virtually every area of the world. The Americans themselves exercised pressure on the British government. Though Churchill had strongly opposed the idea that the British could "pick

The life of Vinayak Damodar Savarkar was uncannily interwoven with that of Gandhi. Savarkar was born in 1883 in Maharashtra to a family of *chitpavan* Brahmins (literally, "purified by fire"). That is, he was a member of that aristocracy of Mahratta Brahmins, like Gokhale and Tilak, who proudly claimed the merit of having bravely opposed the British. In a previous historical period, in the seventeenth century, the Mahratta had rebelled against the Muslims in a kind of Hindu Crusade, under the guidance of a great leader, Shivaji.

Police reports speak of a Savarkar who at the age of ten, ran off to throw stones against the village mosque, after hearing of the Hindu-Muslim battles in the United Provinces. Six years later, the hanging of two terrorists in Maharashtra led him to pledge his life to driving out the British. Together with his older brother, Ganesh, he founded an association of young nationalist, anti-Muslim Brahmins. His idols were Shivaji and Mazzini (Mazzini as "terrorist," not as the author of *The Duties of Man*, which Gandhi admired); he translated a biography of Mazzini into Marathi.

As a student at Pune, he intensified his activity as political agitator: his fiery speeches earned him the nickname of "Demosthenes" of India. Protected by Tilak, he received a scholarship and went to study in London, at India House, a den of young nationalists. He wrote a history of the Indian Mutiny entitled *The First Indian War of Independence in 1857*. He proclaimed the ineffectiveness of passive resistance, and the necessity for violence and secrecy. He got hold of a manual on how to make bombs, had it reprinted in London and sent it out to a number of revolutionary groups in India and in Indian emigrant communities. He secretly sent to India a number of weapons, as well. He persuaded a young Mahratta, Madanlal Dhingra, to kill a British functionary, probably in revenge for the sentence of life-long exile pronounced shortly before against his brother, Ganesh. In the assassination attempt, which took place on July 2, 1909, a young Indian physician who had tried to save the Englishman lost his life as well. Dhingra, who read in the courtroom a declaration claiming responsibility for his act, was condemned and executed. As for Savarkar, he lived in hiding, but never felt free from the control of the police, who nonetheless lacked sufficient evidence to accuse him.

It was during this period that he first met Gandhi, at a banquet organized by a group of extremists on the occasion of an Indian religious festivity. Gandhi had been in London for just a few days, in order to preach the cause of South African Indians. It was agreed that no one would speak of politics during the banquet; but the two found a way to argue just the same, by referring to the ancient epic poem, *Ramayana*. Gandhi maintained that Rama's final victory represents the victory of truth and peaceful courage over evil and falsity: the Indians could become free only by following his example. Savarkar, on the contrary, held that Rama succeeds in regaining his power only after killing Ravan, a symbol of tyranny and oppression.

Some time later, feeling hounded, Savarkar fled to Paris. But he soon returned to London, purportedly to meet his English woman companion. This imprudence cost him dearly, as he was arrested at Victoria Station in March of 1910: not for the murder of the British functionary, but for sending arms to India. He was extradited to India, put on board a ship and kept under strict surveillance. At Marseilles he attempted a bold escape, but was caught again. After arriving in India he, too, was condemned to life-long exile, for a series of crimes including sedition and complicity in the homicide of an Englishman, who had been killed by one of the pistols sent by Savarkar from London. He thus joined his brother, Ganesh, in the Andaman Islands (the Indians' version of "Devil's Island"). Ten years later, in 1920, a third brother wrote to Gandhi. He had heard that the two were not to be included in an amnesty declared by the British, and asked that they be at least transferred to a locality with a better climate, since their health was in jeopardy. Gandhi wrote several articles in defense of the Savarkar brothers, stating that they had now renounced violence. Of Vinayak Damodar, he wrote that he had known him in London as a patriot and a sincere revolutionary: if he had been in prison for ten years, it was due to his love for India. It is difficult to say to what extent Gandhi's intervention mattered. But it is true that in 1921, V.D. Savarkar was transferred to Yeravda prison, and in 1924 he was sent to the border town of Ratnagiri, Tilak's native town. There he was forbidden to become involved in politics. In reality, he ended up by receiving old and new followers, and published a book, *Hindutva*, which would become the Bible of extreme nationalist Hinduism. In it he expressed the idea of Hindu racial superiority, and his dream of a great empire. He wished to induce Muslims and Christians to reconvert to Hinduism, or else leave India. A religious traditionalist, he was also an admirer of Herbert Spencer, and an advocate for modernization in science and economy, aiming as he did to make India a powerful, well-armed State. During the Ratnagiri years, he was blamed for a series of terrorist acts; but the police never succeeded in incriminating him.

In 1927, Gandhi went to Ratnagiri to make a speech. There he visited Savarkar, who was ill, and expressed his respect for the extremist in spite of their differences. The two men once again came up against them while discussing the problem of conversions. At the end of their talk, Gandhi said he recognized their disagreement on many points, but he hoped Savarkar would "have no objection" to his making some "experiments." Savarkar replied by citing the fable of the children and the frogs. Gandhi, he said, would make his "experiments" at the expense of the nation.

Later, Savarkar violently attacked Gandhi several times. In 1937, he gained complete

freedom, and moved to Pune, the ancestral city of the *chitpavan* Brahmins. His followers welcomed him with the name of Vir ("the valorous"); and the Hindu Mahasabha, the Hindu extremist party, elected him president. Savarkar also founded a secret, militarized "Sect of the Hindu Nation," of which he became "dictator," demanding total and blind submission. During the years of tragic conflict between Hindus and Muslims, while Gandhi was desperately struggling to avoid massacres and the dismemberment of the nation, Savarkar (in the words of his biographer) was "ready, like Lincoln, to face a civil war." He fanned the flames.

When Gandhi was killed on January 30, 1948, his assassins were discovered to be *chitpavan* Brahmins, close collaborators and fanatical disciples of Savarkar. The latter was personally implicated by a "repentant" witness, but he stubbornly and cleverly defended himself, and was acquitted for lack of evidence.

He was to die in his bed, at the age of ninety-three, in 1966, and he would be honored in an imposing funeral ceremony. At his funeral, Indira would define him as "a great figure of contemporary India"; and S.A. Dange, president of the Communist Party, would call him "one of the great anti-imperialist revolutionaries." ■

Vinayak Damodar Savarkar, second from left in front row, with fez and glasses, photographed with some of his followers. In the middle we see Nathuram Godse, the extremist who in 1948 would kill Gandhi with three gunshots.

A photo of the historical conference held in New Delhi in June 1947, in which the British plan for the partition of India was accepted. Lord Mountbatten (center) between Nehru (left) and Jinnah. The fourth figure is head of the cabinet for the viceroy, Lord Ismay.
© Publifoto

up their heels and go," liquidating their Empire, the Labour Party government of Clement Attlee, who succeeded him, soon appeared to be more anxious to get away from the Indian peninsula than to prolong the obvious agony.

The problem now facing Indian politicians was the conflict between Congress and the Muslim League. The latter had grown stronger by now: in the first post-war elections it won ninety percent of the seats in Parliament reserved for the Muslim electorate. In the increasingly vain search for a compromise acceptable to both, the British attempted new negotiations and tried concocting new socio-political mixtures; but the mutual suspicion, rancor, and intransigence of the adversaries now doomed all attempts to failure. In August of 1946, the League decided to "say good-bye to constitutional methods" and pass on to "direct action." That was the beginning of a series of bloody riots and massacres between the two communities — first in Calcutta, and then in other cities and provinces. One person bitterly observed that although the Muslim League had never fought against the British, it was now declaring war on Hindus.

During the emergency Nehru was given the task of forming an interim government. A few representatives of the League consented to participate in it for a short time, but they then boycotted the government, condemning it to paralysis.

In February of 1947 the Attlee government announced

that by the following year, power would be transferred into "responsible Indian hands" — that is, to a government demonstrably able to maintain order. The British were by now determined to accelerate independence proceedings, and took for granted the idea that partition of the country into two countries was inevitable. Lord Mountbatten, a cousin of the king and former supreme commander of the resident forces in Southeast Asia, arrived in Delhi as the last Viceroy of British India.

But meanwhile, the country was thrown into chaos by civil war. Sikhs, Hindus, and Muslims were fighting one another in Punjab. Hindus and Muslims were massacring each other in other regions of India. Violence, rape, and forced conversions were everyday affairs. Nevertheless, it was decided that independence would be proclaimed at midnight on August 14.

So it was that two independent dominions were born: India and Pakistan. Lord Mountbatten passed from being viceroy to occupying the post of first governor-gen-

Moving a wounded man during the Calcutta riots in August 1946.
© Publifoto

eral of India; in Pakistan, the mistrustful Jinnah kept this title for himself. A commission headed by an English magistrate was in charge of establishing the borders, through work carried out in secret. This was a particularly delicate task, because in many cases, the new borders cut through districts and villages, dividing families that had lived elbow-to-elbow for centuries. Punjab and Bengal were divided in two: East Bengal became the eastern part of Pakistan (a few years later it would gain independence and become Bangladesh). All of the princely states except three joined one or another of the two new countries; the three exceptions were Kashmir, Hyderabad, and Junagadh, whose populaces were divided by religion, and whose sovereigns pro-

fessed a different faith from that of the majority of their
subjects. As the historian Wolpert points out, bureaucracy and the armed forces had to be dismembered
"from one day to the next," as did the railways, police,
and revenue service; and it was also necessary to divide up trucks, packets of paper, pens and pencils, ru-
pees and pounds. It is hard to imagine the terror and
anguish of millions of Hindus, Sikhs, and Muslims who
feared waking up one morning trapped in a nation hostile to their faith. Many were forced to take up the little
they could carry, and leave their houses and their fields.

In fact, the transfer of power from one group to another was accompanied by a tragedy of biblical pro-
portions. Particularly in provinces where violence had
burst forth in its cruelest forms, masses of Hindus
abandoned their dwellings and moved toward India;

masses of Muslims moved toward Pakistan. It is estimated that Partition created ten million refugees, and a million deaths. More than a third of the Muslims, at any rate, remained in India. In the meantime, a war broke out in Kashmir between India and Pakistan; it was undeclared, but none the less bloody for that. And it was the first of a series.

A few hours before midnight on August 14, Nehru gave a speech at the constitutional assembly in Delhi, which was destined to become famous. It began with these words: "Long years ago we made a tryst with destiny, and now the time comes when we shall redeem our pledge... At the stroke of the midnight hour, when the world sleeps, India will awake to life and freedom." But as he thus proclaimed the end of an era, Nehru's spirit was embittered (as he would later confide) by the image of a

Gandhi in Calcutta, September 1947, shortly before beginning a fast "unto death," which would enable him to obtain a truce in the fighting between Hindus and Muslims.
© Publifoto

One of the last photos of Gandhi, picturing him while going to a prayer assembly at Birla House, in Delhi, on January 29, 1948. The day after, the Mahatma would be assassinated at the same place and in similar circumstances. The two young women wearing glasses on whom Gandhi is leaning are Abha and Manu, orphaned daughters of his relatives; he had virtually adopted them. They were beside the Mahatma even at the moment of his assassination.

divided and tormented India. As for Gandhi, he refused to join in the festivities. The next day, he declared, India would be free of the British yoke. But from midnight on, India would be dismembered. The day after would be a day of joy, but also a day of mourning.

Gandhi had tried in every way to oppose partition, even when it was accepted as the lesser evil by Nehru and by other leaders in Congress. In order to save the unity of the country, he was willing to turn the government over to the Muslims. He would consent to a division of the country, but by a free choice on the part of its inhabitants: once the British had gone, and not under threat of violence. His vision of an independent India was that of a federation of village communities, characterized by widely-shared power, in which it would be possible to accept and appreciate all differences. He thought that once the explosion of intolerance and violence had waned, it would be possible to re-establish peaceful coexistence. Nehru, on the contrary, was driven by the ambition to build a strong, centralized state. He resigned himself to partition, in a sort of desolate realism, when he came to feel that amputation was the price to pay for the compact unity of a new Indian state.

In his last years, it seemed to Gandhi that the madness of humanity had compromised everything to which he had dedicated his entire existence. On January 2, 1947, he said that he felt surrounded by darkness. Between the end of 1946 and the beginning of 1947, he spent four months journeying up and down Bengal and Bihar on foot, like a desperate pilgrim of peace, trying to stop the massacres. He recited verses from the Qur'an in Hindu temples, drawing onto himself the wrath of orthodox Hindus and extremist nationalists. In September, in Calcutta, he began a fast "unto death," thus succeeding in interrupting the violence between Hindus and Muslims in the most populous and violent city of India. He fasted again, for the sake of unity among the religious communities, in Delhi the following January. But with dramatic clarity, he saw his efforts fall to pieces against invincible barriers. In times past, Muslims had joined in listening to him, and had become his disciples; this now occurred more and more rarely. He became the target of attacks from Hindu extremists and groups of refugees, exasperated by the violence they had suffered, and sickened by his words of peace. On January 20, a bomb exploded in the Delhi house where he was a guest, leaving him unhurt. (Six months earlier,

Gandhi's ashes are thrown into the Ganges at Barrackpore.

he had escaped from a terrorist attack against a train on which he was riding.) A few days later he was killed by a young Hindu fanatic hidden in the crowd that was awaiting him in a garden for his evening prayer meeting. As he fell, he pronounced the words *Hej Rama*, the name of God. The conspiracy to which his assassin belonged accused Gandhi, who had done so much to unify India, of having granted too much to the Muslims. The day was January 30, 1948. His ashes were scattered in the Ganges.

Gandhi never had what one would call a true private life. He married at a very young age, but lived for long periods of time away from his wife. Later, he led his family to join the communal life of his South African and Indian *ashrams*, and in 1906 took a vow of *brahmacharya*, putting it into practice with astonishing rigor and willpower. Many aspects of Gandhi's intimate life, and of his relationship to the theory of non-violence, have intrigued students of psychoanalysis.

Gandhi's wife, Kasturbai, was not highly educated, but she was tenacious and patient. Gandhi would have liked to find in her a companion who would wholeheartedly share his goals and aspirations, but in this respect he was partly disappointed. Kasturbai often found it difficult to live the life chosen by her husband; she always remained nostalgically attached to the idea of a "normal" family, which she tried to create, at least in appearance. A dedicated wife, she accepted a quiet, discreet position for herself, leaving to other women of the *ashram* the more ambitious and responsible role of intellectual collaborators of Mohandas. When speaking about her to Romain Rolland, Miss Slade defined her a bit cattily as "a woman for interiors." But on numerous occasions she par-

ticipated in her husband's battles, and she, too, went to prison. Her death in 1944 caused Gandhi immense pain. Gandhi was a severe father. Erikson wrote that he "demanded the best and expected the worst" from his sons — and they knew it. He did not send them to school, because he wanted to educate them himself, together with the other children in the *ashram*. He wanted to forge them into pure fighters for his cause. But in fact, as he himself later admit-

ted, Gandhi was able to dedicate very little time and energy to their education. His sons complained of having been deprived of opportunities offered to other children their age; one or two of them decided to remedy this, at least in part, by taking up regular studies. It was not surprising, then, that Gand-

hi was sometimes disappointed even by his sons; on more than one occasion he felt betrayed by them. Although they all participated in his struggles on occasion — especially in the beginning — only the younger two, Ramdas and Devadas, followed him to the end with some degree of faithfulness, though not without disagreement and difficult moments. Manilal was sent by his father to South Africa to direct the newspaper, *Indian Opinion*, and he spent nearly all the rest of his life there in the loneliness of exile. He was in South Africa when Gandhi was assassinated, and was not even able to attend the funeral.

The life of the first-born, Harilal, deeply loved by his mother, was truly tragic. A rebellious spirit, he enrolled at the university and married against the wishes of his father. The death of his young wife, followed by the death of a son, cruelly wounded his personality, driving him to alcoholism and a dissolute life. He let himself become involved with unscrupulous individuals. Finally, he converted to Islam in a supreme act of defiance of his father, who was deeply embittered, and who painfully had to disassociate himself from his son in public. Having become a sort of tramp, he died of tuberculosis in a Bombay hospital, four months after the assassination of his father (whose funeral he had witnessed as one of many in the crowd).

None of the sons left anything written concerning his relationship with his father. Gandhi always blamed himself for his sons' behavior, when it seemed deplorable to him. And in the last years, he treated them with an affection they had never before known, or been able to recognize, subject as it had been to his conception of self-control. Gandhi was too much a father of all to be father to his sons; as Kasturbai put it one day, "Bapu is a saint, but he has to think of the whole world."

It has been noted that an excessive openness toward the external world, radical non-violence, and the manifestation of ideals of peace and universal love, left in his intimates (especially in his children) an anguish of abandonment, a feeling of desertion and lack of protection. It is also probable that such an extremely lofty role model only left his sons to the difficult alternatives of rebellion, frustration and, compromise.

Toward the end of his life Gandhi was the protagonist in an episode which at the time produced a bit of a scandal (albeit attenuated by the veneration surrounding him). It has created great perplexity in those who have considered it. During the years 1946 and 1947, the Mahatma, seventy by now, was tired and weak, and deeply anguished over the Hindu-Muslim conflict, to whose difficult solution he dedicated his last remaining energy. It was in that period that one of his collabora-

tors found him in bed one morning with his young niece Manubehn, for whom he acted as both father and mother, now that Kasturbai had died. They were both nude, and they were speaking to each other. It turned out that similar episodes had occurred during the same period, with other young women followers.

The story soon got around and was publicly discussed, as had always been the case for every aspect of Gandhi's life. The Mahatma denied having violated his duties as *brahmacharin*. He gave several different explanations, none very clear. They ranged from the need to be helped to overcome the physical and moral coldness that was tormenting him, to the attempt to carry out a grand religious experiment destined to make him into a "eunuch of God," a completely bisexual being, gifted with the innocence of a child. What's more, those

nearest Gandhi had always been struck by the feminine element in the type of seduction exercised by him, and by a sort of desire for maternity, which he seemed to express. The episode remains mysterious. Some people were upset by it, and distanced themselves from Gandhi, while others accused him at the very least of imprudence and extravagance; still others accepted his explanations, which were made believable by the seriousness and sincerity with which they were given.

It was generally only the Western biographers (often with poorly-concealed smiles of irony) who gave much thought to the matter. The Indians tended to be indifferent. What is most salient in the whole incident, given the necessary respect, is the ambiguity that characterizes it. This ambiguity should lead us to recognize certain risks and contradictions, such as the one often marking a relationship between a Master and his faithful (independently of the rightness of a "doctrine") in situations of emotional tension, particularly when the disciples are women, and the risks of exploitation increase. Or perhaps the incident shows the dramatic inconsistency that may arise out of excessively rigid solutions to the problem of sexuality. ■

Left, Kasturbai with four of her sons, in a photo taken around 1903. Above, Gandhi with his god-daughters Abha and Manu.

Chapter 4

INDIA AFTER
INDEPENDENCE

INDEPENDENCE FINDS A DIVIDED AND UNDER-DEVELOPED
COUNTRY TORMENTED BY CONFLICTS THAT THREATEN ITS UNITY.
BUT A GREAT AND VARIED CULTURAL TRADITION, AND GREAT
POTENTIAL, MAKE INDIA TODAY AN ECONOMICALLY AND SOCIALLY
BURGEONING NATION.

P ractically speaking, Indian political life in the five decades following independence has gone through three main phases. The first of these was dominated by the figure of Jawaharlal Nehru, whom Gandhi himself had chosen, in 1946, as the first prime minister of independent India, and who occupied that position until his death in 1964.

A native of Punjab, born into a rich and cultured family of Brahmins, Nehru was the son of Motilal, a lawyer and leader of Congress. In both roles he followed in his father's footsteps. Nehru had been the disciple of Mahatma Gandhi, although the two men were very different; Nehru was a secular politician, a refined, westernized intellectual and writer; Gandhi, on the other hand, was a religious spirit gifted with great charisma. Nehru had studied at Harrow and Trinity College at Cambridge. In the twenties and thirties, during his travels in Europe, he had alternated winter vacations in Switzerland (it was in a Swiss clinic that he received the painful news of the death of his young wife) with participation in several of the great anti-Fascist assemblies in Europe.

He had also been in Barcelona, though only for a short time, during the Spanish Civil War. There he had witnessed a clash between civilizations that endangered the values which he most admired in European culture. A socialist and reformer, profoundly influenced

Street peddlers with a skyscraper in the background; Bombay. This is one of the contrasts enriching contemporary India, a continually evolving country — still backward in many sectors, but at the vanguard in others, from computer technology to nuclear power.

by Fabian theories, he did not conceal his admiration for the Soviet experiment (and in this he resembled many British socialists of his time). He wanted to see for himself how the Soviet experiment was proceeding. He was active in India for nearly three decades, working at Gandhi's side or, occasionally, in conflict with him; he was imprisoned many times, and for many years. Now, at the age of fifty-eight, this fascinating and tenacious man, who always wore a red rose pinned to his white jacket, found himself facing the difficult task of building an independent state containing 350 million inhabitants.

A late Victorian portrait of the gentleman, Motilal Nehru, posing with his wife, Swaruprani, and son, Jawaharlal. Years later it will be the latter's turn to pose for the photographer, with his wife, Kamala, and little Indira (right).
© Publifoto

National Unity

Beginning in 1947, the new Indian leaders found themselves facing the task of consolidating a unity which old and new factors were rendering precarious. In the first place there was the lack of a united tradition, compensated only in part by the function performed by anti-British nationalism in cultivating a sense of community. And there was (as there still is today) an incredible variety of languages and religious denominations. This sea of divergence and disunity led to the first great choice by Nehru and his collaborators: that of federalism. India assumed the name of the Indian Union, Bharat Juktarashtra. Bharat, in Sanskrit, is the name of the first Aryan who, according to legend, unified the subcontinent.

Nehru wanted the central power of the Union to be strong enough, however, to counterbalance the autonomy of the single states. Each of these was granted its own legislative assembly and government, headed by a "Chief Minister." But the central government maintained power of control and intervention, as well as exclusive responsibility in matters of general interest, such as defense, foreign policy, and communications.

A significant element of this power is the so-called Presidential rule: the president's right, in the case of serious political instability, to dissolve a local legislative assembly and to pass control of a state into the hands of central government. The central government has exercised this right more than once, often with painful consequences. It must also be remembered that the Indian constitution does not allow for the existence of different nationalities or ethnic and linguistic minorities, but only of individuals enjoying the same rights, independently of the group they belong to. The kind of practical politics which has developed during the following decades has done more to favor the power of central government than has the constitution; though, in any case, the regions have found a good measure of free expression.

Today, the Union comprises twenty-five states and seven territories directly administered by the central government. At first, the states were in the minority. But in many cases, separate ethnic and linguistic groups cohabited in the same state, or else the same ethnic group was divided up between more than one state. From this situation, despite Nehru's initial opposition, claims arose which led to the dismemberment of some states and the birth of others which were more compact from a linguistic or ethnic point of view. Even today, demands for autonomy are causing tension and conflict.

National unity had always been one of Nehru's major preoccupations: to the extent, as we have seen, that he was led to accept Partition in exchange for a more vital, cohesive country, even though its size was reduced.

In the first years after independence, unity was also completed and consolidated by military means. One military operation, as early as 1948, resolved the problem of the giant Hyderabad, a princely state whose sovereign (the *nizam*) had delayed joining the Union. Another armed intervention a few years later restored the territory of Goa to India, after fruitless negotiations with the Portuguese (while, on the contrary, the French agreed to pull out of Pondicherry and its other Indian possessions peacefully).

Alongside the creation of a federal political system with a strong central government, independent India chose a Western-style democratic system. Suffrage was extended to all adult citizens: in 1951 there were 173 million voters, which made India "the largest democracy in the world."

Secularism

In the area of relations between the State and religion, Nehru defended a decidedly secular concept (as Gandhi had done). It can be summed up in the formula according to which the State treats all religions equal-

HINDUS, HINDUIST, AND INDIANS

The term **Hinduist** specifically refers to a person embracing the religion of Hinduism. The much more commonly-used word, **Hindu**, on the other hand, emphasizes the diverse set of creeds, cultures, traditions, and social customs connected with Hinduism. But since Hinduism is a religion permeating culture, daily life, and social life in its entirety, the two terms tend to become synonymous.

The meaning of Indian, on the other hand, implied a different context. This word has an essentially geographical connotation designating simply the inhabitants of the Indian nation. In most cases, Indians are also Hindus, but there are Muslim Indians, Parsi Indians, and Christian Indians, too. Only a few nationalist Hindu groups maintain that being Indian necessarily means being Hindu (one reason why they are hostile to the presence of Muslims in the country). It must be kept in mind that Hinduism is not an evangelical religion: it has never tried to make converts outside India. It therefore tends to be the religion of a people: you are born a Hindu, you do not become one. Orthodox Hinduism considers Buddhists, Jains, and Sikhs to be follow-ers of Hinduist currents of thought, and not members of independent religions (though Buddhists and Sikhs generally disagree with this interpretation).

The origin of the both the words "India" and "Hindu" is quite curious. A Sanskrit word, *sindhu*, generally indicated waterways, and the Indus River in particular. The ancient Persians and the Greeks, and then the Muslims, used this word to designate the peoples living in the lands beyond the Indus, and it was only a few centuries ago that the Indians themselves began adopting it, accepting it from outside. ∎

ly. This principle, confirmed in the Indian Constitution, was opposed by advocates of "communalism:" who wanted an important political role for religious "communities." As the historian Zins notes, the "secularists" were those who unlike the "communalists" refused to exploit membership in a given religious community for political purposes. The wounds opened by Partition were, at any rate, difficult to heal; in fact, they have never totally healed. The rivalry between Hindus and Muslims continued to smolder dangerously, in spite of the efforts of most leaders of Congress, as well as leaders from other parties, to make peace. Both Muslims and Sikhs came to occupy some of the highest public offices in the new nation.

The 1950 Constitution did not touch on the problem of castes, but it did abolish untouchability. Nevertheless, the *harijan* problem remained an unsolved one in Indian society.

The Economy

In the area of economic development, Nehru was inspired by a democratic socialism which aimed to reconcile strong state intervention with private initiative. The declared goals were, predictably enough, fighting hunger and famine, and giving form to a modern national economy. These objectives were hindered by the backward conditions prevailing at the birth of independent India, as well as the lack of capital, energy sources, and infrastructures.

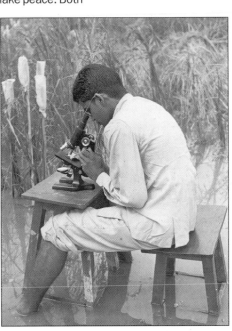

A student at the center for hybrid rice, at Cuttack, Orissa, in 1958. This is one of the numerous institutes for agrarian studies promoted by the FAO.
© Publifoto

Many sectors were reserved for the state (the military industry, nuclear energy, railways), or at least placed under state control (mines, the steel industry, shipbuilding, aeronautics, oil, telecommunications). It was the entrepreneurial bourgeoisie of India that favored this choice. This class was characterized by a high concentration of capital in the hands of a few dom-

Voters lining up in Calcutta for the first general elections of independent India, January, 1952.
© 2 Publifoto

On the right, Nehru, the first Prime Minister of India, just before his death in 1964.

inant families: the Tatas, the Birlas, the Godrejes, to name the most prominent.

The Tata family, a Parsi family who pioneered Indian industry during the nineteenth century, possessed a financial empire of incredibly vast and varied dimensions. This bourgeoisie looked with favor upon a strong state presence in those sectors which, requiring high and risky investments without the prospect of immediate profit, would have been neglected by private initiative. The Indian capitalist bourgeoisie was therefore supported by a numerous and powerful class of administrators and technicians who managed the state sector (and who were often accused of inefficiency, bureaucratism, and corruption). The relationship between these two strata — private capitalists and state administrators — oscillated between cooperation and competition.

In the area of agriculture, the fifties were witness to some attempts at agrarian reform which, unfortunately, remained largely theoretical, or were thwarted by the political power of rich farmers. The relative failure of these reforms (while results obtained in the area of industrial progress, on the contrary, were quite successful, even in the early years) kept Indian agriculture in a depressed state for many years, and slowed down the battle against the hunger and misery of the peasant masses. But the "green revolution," which began in 1971, finally brought important results. Based on the use of high-yield varieties of rice and wheat, it involved considerable investment in irrigation works, machinery, chemical fertilizers, and pesticides. The "green revolution" focused on several areas which had rich good soil as well as entrepreneurs — above all, Punjab, but also Uttar Pradesh and Haryana. As it was applied to only twenty percent of the agrarian sector, it had the negative side effect of widening geographic and social disparities, which caused protest demonstrations on the part of many peasants.

However, it cannot be denied that the "green revolution" brought good results in the struggle against hunger and famine, which justified attempts to extend it further. Indeed, it is partly because of these reforms that agricultural output nearly tripled from 1950 until today.

Political Life

The years between 1947 and 1964 were not only dominated by the figure of Nehru, but also by the electoral supremacy of the Congress Party. Growing from 630,000 members in 1936 to seventeen million in 1950, during the Nehru era Congress never obtained less than forty percent of votes in national elections, and always held the absolute majority of seats in Parliament. Moreover, it governed many areas of the single Union states.

This supremacy was, however, threatened by several rivals. To the right of Congress stood the Hindu Mahasabha ("Great Hindu Assembly"), founded in 1914, which also boasted an armed wing, the RSS (Rashtriya Swayamsevak Sangh, "National Organization of Hindu Volunteers"), founded in 1925, and outlawed for some time —after one of its members killed Gandhi — though later it was legalized again. It was precisely these two extremist traditionalist organizations, with their

religious affiliations, that in 1951 founded the Jan Sangh party, whose latest incarnation is the present Bharatiya Janata Party ("Indian People's Party").

To the left of Congress stood the Communist Party. It was illegal in the early years following independence because it was linked to several guerrilla actions, which the government put down by force. Having officially returned to the political arena, the Communist Party nonetheless remained torn by internal conflict that in 1964 led to its split into the pro-Soviet Indian Communist Party and the pro-Chinese Indian Marxist Communist Party. Later, in 1967, a third party, the Marxist-Leninist Communist Party, rose out of the peasant-student insurrection of the "Naxalites" (named after the locality of Naxalbari, in Bengal, where it broke out).

The fulcrum of political conflict, however, lay within Congress. As heir to the struggle for independence, it represented everyone: landowners, entrepreneurs, artisans, city intellectuals, and also peasants. Its members and electorate were predominantly Hindus, but also included Sikhs and Muslims. And it was only to be expected that this variety of interests would correspond to a variety of contrasting positions. Such conflict helps to explain, for example, the hesitancy and inefficacy of the party's attempts to reform land ownership.

Contrasts

Shortly after independence, Nehru and Patel, the powerful minister of internal affairs and one of the most highly-respected leaders in Congress, found themselves alternating between close collaboration with each other and rather open opposition. For example, they cooperated in facing and solving problems about the nation's unity. Patel and Nehru both agreed to end the problem of the princely states through tough military intervention.

On the other hand, the two differed in their attitudes toward economic choices, and toward "communalism." Nehru advocated centralized planning with heavy state intervention in the economy; and he maintained a rigorous "secularism" in the face of the various religious communities. Patel, instead, had little sympathy for socialism and was inclined to maintain cordial relations with traditionalist Hindus. Patel's death in 1950 did not eliminate these divisions from the heart of the Congress Party, but Nehru did manage to impose his influence and political line. On the whole, the Nehru years were ones of great political stability.

Left, communist demonstration in New Delhi, 1963; below, Sardar *Vallabhbhai Patel, minister of Internal Affairs under Nehru.*
© 2 Publifoto

Nehru's prestige diminished somewhat during the last two years of his government (and of his life), which were embittered by criticism of his economic decisions, and above all, India's severe politico-military failure in the 1962 war with China. After Nehru died he was succeeded by an old follower of Gandhi, L.B. Shastri, who in turn died two years later in Tashkent, immediately after concluding a pact meant to stop the armed conflict with Pakistan.

The Indira Gandhi Years

After the brief interim period of Shastri's government, a second phase began in the history of independent India: the Indira Gandhi phase. The Nehru dynasty

The young Indira Gandhi photographed together with the Mahatma in 1935.
© Publifoto

started up anew. In 1966, at the age of thirty-nine, Indira Gandhi was elected premier of the second most populated country in the world. She was the granddaughter of Motilal and beloved only child of Jawaharlal, but she was not related in any way to the Mahatma: her surname came to her through marriage to a politician, Feroze Shah Gandhi, who died an early death in 1960, leaving her two sons, Rajiv and Sanjay.

Indira completed her studies at Santiniketan, the ashram-university headed by Tagore; then in Switzerland and at Oxford. She worked for a long period beside her father, and held a ministerial post in Shastri's government, though this is hardly enough to explain her rapid ascent in the face of aggressive competition. But she soon revealed traits of intelligence and courage, ambition and open-mindedness. It is difficult not to interpret her determination that her sons follow in her footsteps as a sign of strong dynastic ambition. Rajiv disappointed her at first, since he gave precedence to his private choices over politics. He became an airplane pilot, and married an Italian girl, Sonia Maino. The younger Sanjay, instead, soon became the leader of Congress Youth, and seemed destined to occupy important roles; but he died in 1980, at the young age of thirty-three, when the airplane he was flying crashed. At this point it was Rajiv's turn to embrace the political life, and suddenly, to take the place of his mother, in the wave of emotion caused by her violent death. Rajiv himself died in a terrorist attack by Tamil extremists in 1991. In seeking a successor, Congress turned to his widow before considering any one else. Wisely, she declined.

The Nehru-Gandhi dynasty was not merely one phase in the history of modern India, but encompassed several different phases. It can be said that the second phase started with Indira Gandhi's election, and ended nine years later, in 1975, with the emergency laws.

As prime minister, Indira Gandhi followed the political goals conceived by her father, even aiming to accelerate their achievement by way of stronger central control over social and economic life. She heightened the managerial and protectionist tendencies of Nehru; she nationalized the banks. But she was also heir to the many problems that had already appeared in the last two years of her father's life. She had to face the Congress Party's first, worrisome electoral losses, and a violent battle for power within the party that ended with a division. However, Indira Gandhi managed to win out over her opponents, succeeded in limiting damage caused by the split, and in 1971, in the elections that followed, she won an enormous victory. She was by now enormously popular, even charismatic: identified with the "mother goddess" of Indian tradition, she became the object of a true personality cult. But at the same time, the contradictions shaking Indian society and politics were becoming more and more acute. The "socialist" Indira's desire for reforms had already caused splits in Congress. And for the first time, Congress was no longer able to contain and mediate the conflict between reformers and conservatives. A liberal-conservative party, the Swatantra Party, which had existed since 1959, grew in popularity. Beginning in 1973, in an open challenge to Indira Gandhi and Congress and in the wake of a popular "Gandhian socialist" named Jayaprakash Narayan, a heterogeneous coalition began forming which comprised conservatives from Swatantra and the minority wing of Congress, the Hindu nationalist right, new regional formations, and even (though with some hesitation) Marxist Communists. The name that the coalition chose for itself was Janata ("People"). The battle be-

came tough, and both sides used every weapon available. Indira Gandhi was accused of maintaining a personal power structure, now shared only with a restricted group of advisers (of whom her son, Sanjay, was one of the foremost). The Supreme Court, for its part, came on the scene by invalidating the election of Indira Gandhi to Parliament.

The State of Emergency

In 1975, Indira Gandhi responded to the many attacks against her by declaring a state of emergency. She theorized a "disciplined democracy," arrested her opponents (at the end of the emergency period, nearly 40,000 people had been incarcerated), suspended civil rights, and extended preventive detention to a period of two years; she tried to bend the magistrates, who were hostile to her, to the political power; she replaced the political class with a State bureaucracy; she shut down some newspapers, and censored others; she declared that the primary function of radio is to "explain the posi-

Indira with her two sons, Rajiv and Sanjay, in the garden of her home in Delhi, October 1967.
© Publifoto

tion of the government." Sanjay assumed a more and more prominent and disquieting role. Among other things, he generated hate and fear because of the way in which he directed a birth control campaign: apparently, he did not even shrink from forced sterilization.

In many ways, it was a strange dictatorship. For one thing, it was a rare case of a "dictatorship of the center," as the French scholar, Zins, defined it. In 1975 Indira Gandhi found herself at a crossroads. Social conflict had grown more and more acute. Congress no longer possessed the capacity for mediation that had for years allowed it to conduct a political course which, although pragmatic and opportunistic, was essentially center-left. Indira Gandhi could have moved further left by asking for communist support (or at least, for support from the Indian Communist Party, which remained by her side during the emergency); but she chose not to. Or she might have surrendered the government to the right; but this, too, she refused to do. She thus chose a populist, authoritarian solution, in the vain attempt to follow a political course which no longer had either a base or social consensus. Significantly, during the two years of the emergency period, Indira Gandhi's policy aimed above all to reassure the business community, as well as national and international investors. And significantly, while closing their eyes (after a moment of hesitation) to Indira Gandhi's mutilation of democracy, those sectors were generous in their support of her.

Even among Indira Gandhi's critics, there are those who maintain that she acted legally. They say that she faced a real emergency by finding all she needed in the subclauses and fine print of the constitution and laws. The scope and dimension of her coup d'état make such an interpretation hard to swallow. But the fact remains that two years later, when Indira Gandhi held new elections, and lost them, she accepted the punishment with a sense of discipline. She surrendered her power to the heterogeneous coalition that had threatened her, before its leaders ended up in prison or under house arrest. Therein was a victory of the "greatest democracy in the world."

A poster put up throughout the country during the emergency. In referring to the words of the poster, a politician of the opposition ironically commented that Indira had "saved the republic by turning it into a monarchy."
© Publifoto

But it was a pyrrhic victory for the Janata coalition. In no time at all, it fell to pieces, its cohesiveness destroyed, once traditionalism, liberalism, and libertarian socialism discovered they could no longer cohabit. Morarji Desai, one of Indira Gandhi's most implacable adversaries, barely managed to hang on to his position at the head of the new government: in 1979, old and ill, he handed in his resignation and retired from political life. Elections were held again the same year.

Disappointed by the coalition experience, the Indian electorate again chose Indira Gandhi (though with no real enthusiasm). Once again, she became prime minister. She would remain in this role until 1984, when she was shot down by two Sikhs.

The Third Phase

The last years of Indira Gandhi's government (like those of Desai's) now belonged to a new phase, the third one, which has continued up to this day. These years have been characterized by the gradual adoption of neo-liberal measures and by the dismemberment of statism — tendencies which intensi-

fied in the eighties and nineties. Most importantly the fundamental realities of Indian political life changed. Congress, the great party that had dominated the scene for nearly three decades, stood by and watched much of its power waste away. The stability of the Nehru years gave way to chronic instability: there were only three governments during the thirty period from 1947 to 1977, and seven in the fifteen years that followed. Congress remained the most important party, and formed other governments: with Rajiv Gandhi in 1984, and with Narasimha Rao in 1992. It no longer had an absolute majority, and was continually forced to look for compromise and new alliances. For its part, the opposition, too, was fragmented. It was made up of movements and parties that changed names, formed and reformed. The Janata coalition, which resumed its government activities in 1989–1991, continued to pay the price of its eclecticism and internal divisions, as it had in 1979. The regionalist parties gained, offering disquieting evidence of a nation growing apart. Today these parties

On the left, two opponents of Indira Gandhi, Jayaprakash Narayan above and below, Moraji Desai, Prime Minister of India 1977–79
© 2 Publifoto

are present in numerous state governments, while the Marxist Communists have almost continuously governed Bengal and Kerala, performing their own kind of regional role.

In the absence of great acknowledged leaders, a new political class came onstage, sometimes composed of ex-movie actors, such as N.T. Rama Rao in Andhra Pradesh and M.G. Ramachandran in Tamil Nadu. Membership in a caste, faction, or lobby played a more and more important part in political life. Contrary to the deepest aspirations of Gandhi and Nehru, religion invaded the field of politics. The popularity of extremist religious parties grew: parties that tended to alternate legal political battles with violent, fanatical mass action.

In late 1992, in the city of Ayodhya, in Uttar Pradesh, a crowd of Hindu nationalists destroyed a mosque that they thought had been built by Muslims in 1528 at the site where Rama was born — Rama, the mythical sov-

Indira Gandhi leaves prison. Shortly after her defeat by the Janata coalition in the elections of March 1977, Indira had managed to re-enter Parliament by winning a second round of elections. The government of Moraji Desai then committed the error of giving her a martyr's halo by having her expelled from Parliament and arrested. But her imprisonment lasted only a week. Thanks partly to the numerous demonstrations from supporters throughout the country; a prelude, in a way, to her return to power.
© Publifoto

ereign who became a divinity, and who is the protagonist of the great epic poem, the *Ramayana*. In the months that followed, Bombay was devastated by bloody explosions of extremist Islamic origin, and then by the massacre of Muslims by fanatical groups of Hindu nationalists.

In the years 1989–1993, clashes between religious groups left thousands dead across the country. Tension remained high in the aftermath as well, exacerbated by the conflict in Kashmir and the persistent hostility between India and Pakistan.

Muslims in prayer at the Jami Masjid, the great mosque in Delhi, on the last day of Ramadan.
© Publifoto

HINDUS AND MUSLIMS:

Conflicts between Hindus and Muslims have a long history. As we have seen, the arrival of Islam in India was the result both of slow, centuries-long, peaceful penetration, and violent waves of invasion. During the era of the Moghul Empire, periods of relative religious peace and tolerance alternated with times of intolerance and persecution, violence and wars. This is part of the explanation of the ferocity that accompanied independence and Partition. (It is impossible to find sufficient explanation, as is often attempted, in the policy of "divide and conquer" adopted by the British with respect to the two communities.)

Recent years have seen an ominous return of violence between Hindus and Muslims, due to growing intolerance, and to both communities' fanatical tendencies which are in such contrast with the peaceful traditions and forces of Indian culture.

Indian Islam itself is a widely diversified world. For cen-

turies much of Indian Islam, especially in the villages, reflected a serene kind of faith: a religion of peace and brotherhood able to live alongside Hinduism. And there were no ethnic or linguistic differences to aggravate religious diversity: in the great majority, the Indian Muslims are descendants of Indian converts to Islam, when they are not actual converts themselves. Moreover, the Indian Muslims are

proud of having participated in the construction of their country. Northern India, beginning with its architecture, abounds with evidence of a great Indo-Islamic culture.

At the same time, Indian Islam has been subject to waves of extremism, ever since the twenties of this century. Its fraternities (*jamaat*) have actively sought converts. In modern years, the violent attack against the writer,

The 1991 elections proceeded in a climate of great violence as well, with hundreds of victims (including Rajiv Gandhi himself) killed by Tamil terrorists. The elections confirmed the Congress Party in its position as holder of a relative majority (one of its leaders, Narasimha Rao, formed a new government); but they also brought an increase in the number of votes given to the Bharatiya Janata Party, an expression of the Hindu nationalist right which was most widely supported in the northern and western states. In the next elections, in 1996, the Bharatiya was confirmed as the

A DIFFICULT CO-EXISTENCE

Salman Rushdie, originated in India itself, even before the Ayatollah Khomeini exploited it in order to use it as a symbol of his power within the Muslim world community. Unlike Islam, Hindu nationalism has an old history, even though it represented a minor trend until recent times. Its roots date back to certain nineteenth-century movements: Tilak, the Hindu Mahasabha, the paramilitary organization RSS (which was temporarily outlawed more than once); or to the Vishva Hindu Parishad ("Universal Hindu Association"), created in 1964 by the RSS, which acts outside the political sphere in order to promote Hinduism. As early as the twenty-year period between the two world wars, the concept of hindutva or "Hinduness" was elaborated, according to which being Indian and being Hinduist are the same thing. This idea gave rise to hostility toward converts to other religions (especially Islam), and the will to force them to reconvert to

their original ethnic religion. It is difficult to speak of "fundamentalism" in relation to a religion which does not "found" itself on sacred scriptures, and whose doctrine has vague, variable borderlines, although some currents of thought tend toward the construction of a Hinduist orthodoxy. Scholars prefer to speak of Hindu nationalism, and to view its recent growth as the result of many forces. One of these is a "majority group's inferiority complex" with respect to other communities which are less numerous but more united and compact — and in some cases, even protected, as minorities, by law and custom. Another is a sort of preventive, aggressive reaction, nurtured on fear, in the face of the Islamic fundamentalism which is burgeoning nearly everywhere. And another, still, is an "indigenist" and "traditionalist" reaction (as in many other movements present in the so-called Third World) against the identity crisis caused by secularization and

westernization. (In India such reactions are more deeply rooted and widespread than elsewhere.) Finally, we find protest against a degraded political life, and against the persistence (in spite of the economic progress which has been made) of extreme poverty.

In the attempt to mobilize masses of the disinherited, the Hindu nationalists exploit ancient rancor resulting from various causes: the centuries of Muslim rule imposed on Hindus in some areas; the "betrayal" wrought by Partition and the founding of Pakistan; and others as well. Xenophobia is certainly one component of these movements. One of them, Shiv Sena or "Shiva's Army" (which in 1995 won the elections in Bombay — today, Mumbai — the metropolis which is the heart of the Indian economy), combines Marattha nationalism, a violent aversion to Islam, and an equally violent hostility to the myriads of immigrants from the poor southern regions. ∎

Right, the destruction of the Ayodhya mosque by Hindu fanatics, in December 1992.
© Sygma/Grazia Neri

major party in the nation, but it was not able to form a government, and so had to give way to a heterogeneous center-left coalition (the National Front-Left Front), presided over by H.D. Deve Gowda and supported by the dramatically weakened Congress. The 1996 elections also confirmed the growth of regional parties.

Unity Threatened

In recent years, the most serious problem that India has found itself facing has been the threat to its unity. Never has Ernest Renan's definition of the nation been more appropriate than today: "A plebiscite that

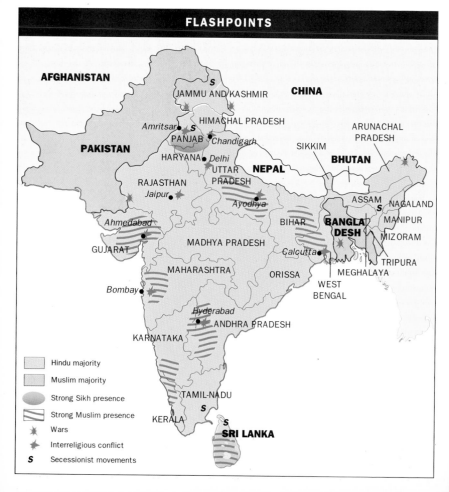

FLASHPOINTS

AFGHANISTAN

JAMMU AND KASHMIR   CHINA

HIMACHAL PRADESH

Amritsar   ARUNACHAL PRADESH

PANJAB Chandigarh

PAKISTAN   SIKKIM

HARYANA Delhi   BHUTAN

UTTAR NEPAL

RAJASTHAN PRADESH

Jaipur   ASSAM NAGALAND

Ayodhya   MANIPUR

Ahmedabad   BIHAR BANGLA DESH MIZORAM

GUJARAT   MADHYA PRADESH

Calcutta   TRIPURA

MAHARASHTRA   ORISSA MEGHALAYA

Bombay   WEST BENGAL

Hyderabad

ANDHRA PRADESH

KARNATAKA

Hindu majority

Muslim majority

Strong Sikh presence   TAMIL-NADU

Strong Muslim presence   KERALA

Wars   SRI LANKA

Interreligious conflict

S Secessionist movements

is renewed from day to day." Many maintain that India is an artificial construction, destined sooner or later to split up into its various components, as happened with the Soviet Union and Yugoslavia. Others, on the contrary, believe that its unity is stronger than its divergences; that the long struggle for independence, and the nearly 50 years of life as a union, have consolidated a common national sentiment, capable of resisting the many centrifugal, disintegrating forces. The optimists also point out the fact, unusual in a Third World country, that democracy has worked, substantially, for half a century (the only exception being the "emergency" of 1975–1977), and that the armed forces have never tried to perform a political role.

But beginning in 1990, the interethnic and interreligious conflicts (especially between Hindus and Muslims), regionalisms, and the persistent separatist and autonomist guerrilla movements, have made the risk of disintegration an everyday threat.

Kashmir, Punjab, and Other Regional Conflicts

Two extremely serious cases of internal conflict are those of Kashmir and Punjab, where for years war has appeared to be almost endemic. Clashes have been harshest in Kashmir.

A mountainous territory occupied in vast

expanses by the Karakorum and the Himalayas, Kashmir looms over the northern entrance to the Indo-Gangetic plain. It is therefore an area of great strate-

*S*ikhs celebrating the death of
Indira Gandhi in the streets of
Southall, in London, on
November 1, 1984.
© Publifoto

gic importance, since it extends over the meeting points
of the Indian, Pakistani, and Chinese borders, approaching Afghanistan and Tajikistan (until recently,
part of the Soviet Union) to the north. Inhabited mostly by Muslims, but governed by a Hindu sovereign at
the moment of independence, its status was bitterly
contested by India and Pakistan (who have fought two
wars over it, in 1948 and 1965). Under the surveillance of the United Nations, it was divided up between
the two countries in 1949; the Indian part today forms
one of the states of the Union, called Jammu and Kashmir, with Srinagar as its capital. A slice of one of its
districts, Ladakh, is occupied by China.

The 1949 partition did not resolve the problem, nor
did it pacify Kashmir. So this region of extraordinary
beauty, which had aspired to become a sort of Asiatic
Switzerland, has never known peace. On the contrary,
tension continued to increase so much that from 1989
on, Kashmir has been the site of persistent guerrilla
warfare, nurtured, too, by Islamic extremism. Once
nearly all the Hindus had emigrated or escaped from
Kashmir proper and the population remaining was nearly all Muslim; today Hindus represent the majority in

the district of Jammu, and Buddhists, in that of Ladakh.

The anti-Indian guerrilla movement was split between advocates of independence for Kashmir, and those favoring its annexation to Pakistan (which more or less openly supported them). The Indian army intervened in full force, with 400,000 soldiers and police. There have since been more than 12,000 victims, and today the situation is one of almost daily violence, terrorist acts, and armed clashes.

Punjab, which lies southwest of Kashmir, was divided in half between India and Pakistan at the moment of independence. It has a predominantly Sikh population (about twelve million out of a total of twenty million inhabitants of that state). It must be remembered that Sikhs do not reside only in Punjab: active and enterprising like few other Indian communities, they are scattered throughout India. Although they represent only two percent of the total national population, they have always occupied important social positions such as high army posts (and a Sikh has been President of the Republic). Furthermore, they are proportionately the most numerous among the Indian emigrant communities in Great Britain, Canada, and the US. Traditional demands for greater autonomy brought about armed conflict in Punjab in the eighties. It was led by a violent, radical movement demanding independence.

In 1984, the Indian army made a bloody invasion into the Golden Temple of Amritsar, a sanctuary of the Sikh faith, where the most fanatical leaders of the movement had taken refuge. During the same year, a group of Sikhs assassinated Prime Minister Indira Gandhi, with the intent of avenging the offense suffered. After the tragic incident, terrorist episodes alternated for years with violent repressive moves by the army and police, causing about 20,000 deaths.

Only in 1992 did there seem to be any real change of direction. The radical movement had by then lost its most prestigious leaders, as well as much of the approval that had once been accorded it by a populace now tired of the violence. The government forces gained ground and, with them, more moderate Sikhs who did not demand independence, but reform. One reform demanded was different distribution of waters taken from

Jammu and Kashmir	65,85%
Assam	24%
West Bengal	20,45%
Uttar Pradesh	19,5%
Bihar	15,5%
Gujarat	13,5%
Karnataka	10,5%
Maharashtra	10,5%
Andhra Pradesh	8,5%
Rajasthan	8,3%
Tripura	6,5%
Manipur	6,5%
Tamil-Nadu	5%
Madhya Pradesh	4,5%

% of Muslim population

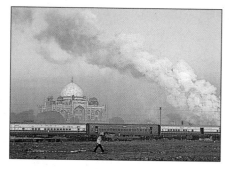

the Indus for irrigation; another, the definitive transfer of the city of Chandigath to Punjab (presently, this city is directly administered by the central government, and functions as capital for both Punjab and the bordering state of Haryana). The situation remains tense, in any case.

Other armed conflicts are present in India today as well. Assam, which once was a vast territory ruled by a maharaja, is now divided into seven states, of which the most populous still bears the original name of the whole territory. In almost all the northeastern states, violent conflicts fester due to many and varied causes. One very serious problem arises from the demands for autonomy made by minority groups of *adivasi*, or "tribals," "original inhabitants," such as the Gurkha and Bodo (whereas other *adivasi*, such as the Naga and Mizo, have obtained autonomy). The Gurkha are of Nepalese origin and warrior traditions (until a few years ago they formed a special regiment of great prestige in the Indian army). They now claim the right to self-government in territories surrounding the city of Darjeeling.

Some peoples living in this area are distinct from the majority of the populace — Indo-European or Dravidic — not only in language (they generally speak languages belonging to the Sino-Tibetan group), but also because they are Christians.

In some states, the native inhabitants react against mass immigration from nearby regions and states (from Bangladesh, above all, but also from Nepal, Myanmar — once Burma — and Bengal). In Assam especially, such reactions have resulted in the bloody massacre of immigrants. Other conflicts have broken out in poor peasant areas where Maoist-inspired protest movements repeat their experiments of the sixties and seventies, which ended in bloody defeat. Autonomist claims giving rise to frequent episodes of violence are present in other states as well, such as Uttar Pradesh and Tamil Nadu. There, as in the south of India the ancient Dravidic culture has risen up to oppose Brahmanic power.

In many of these conflicts, causes of an ethnic, linguistic, cultural, religious, economic, and social nature are not easily distinguishable; they mix in with one another. For example, the immigrants arriving in great numbers in Hindu Assam, rich in tea and oil, are not attacked simply because they are outsiders, but also because they are poor, and in need of work, and — what's more — Muslims. The Sikhs are followers of a religion which is also largely identified with a territory, Punjab. And they have had their own particular history for at least three centuries. Furthermore, their state, Punjab, is one of the richest in India, the one where the Green Revolution met with greatest success. In the early 1980s, Punjab provided seventy-three percent of the national cereal crop and forty-eight percent of the rice. It is therefore easy to understand why the Indian Union is not willing to agree to the secession of this bona fide granary.

Images of India today, poised between tradition and the future.
© 4 Publifoto

A Country of Contrasts

With its enormous land surface, and population second only to China's, India appears a land of contrasts from any possible viewpoint. Geographically, it ranges from the highest mountains on earth to immense plains, and from extreme drought to the most disastrous flooding. And the great contrasts do not touch only on nature; they also mark social life, the economy, and culture.

For a long time, India appeared to its visitors to be a land of overwhelming and indescribable poverty. A land of people starving in miserable villages continually threatened by famine; of beggars, maimed and blind people; of men, women, and children weakened by malnutrition and disease, sitting on sidewalks awaiting death. All of this has not disappeared; it is not just a memory. The poverty of earlier times that had been due to meager crops and the primitive agricultural methods still used in some regions, has been joined by a new, metropolitan poverty. Shantytowns flank the great cities, where millions of people flock, fleeing the fields, with the dream of finding better conditions. Although many battles have been won in the war against hunger, today there are still families living on the sidewalk, and children who are deliberately mutilated (this still happens in Bombay/Mumbai) so that they can become more convincing beggars.

The per capita income is $1,500 or about five per-

THE LANGUAGES OF INDIA

The languages spoken in India, numbering at least a thousand, are divided into two great principal groups: Indo-European in the north, and Dravidic in the south.

As many as thirteen of them are spoken by over 10 million people, and 33, by more than a million. The most widely-spoken is Hindi (spoken by about 30% of Indians), as we can see by this chart from 1981:

Hindi	**264 million**
Telegu	**54 million**
Bengali	**51 million**
Marathi	**49 million**
Tamil	**44 million**
Urdu	**35 million**
Gujarati	**33 million**

After independence, Hindi was established as the official language of India, temporarily flanked by English.

But many states have opposed this solution, claiming the right to use their own language. Thus English continues to be the main vehicle of communication on a national level, although only four per-

cent of Indians are able to read it. For example, many of the major daily newspapers are published in English. But naturally, there are also many papers printed in other Indian languages. ■

cent of the US's and about eight percent of the UKs. Thirty seven percent of Indians live below what is considered to be the poverty line ($180 a year). Illiteracy is slightly lower than fifty percent. Out of 1,000 babies born, even today sixty-nine die during the first year of life, and life expectancy is only sixty years, compared with almost eighty in developed countries. On the average, each physician must care for more than 2,100 potential patients, compared to 381 in the US and 629 in the UK. The situation, however, is changing quite rapidly, and it would be wrong to consider India only as a poor, underdeveloped country. For example, if it is true that the average life span today is 60, only 20 years ago it was 47.3, and ten years ago, 53.3. The percentage of literate women was 29.7 percent ten years ago, while today it has risen to 39.4 percent, with a far higher rate of growth than for men.

A nuclear plant in India. Left, a newsstand in New Delhi.
© Publifoto

If it is true that India remains a poor country in many ways, it is an outstanding leader in others. Scientific research is advanced in the field of physics (including nuclear physics) and mathematics. Besides possessing the atom bomb, India has sent its own satellites into space. Computer technology, in particular, has seen swift development. There are 100,000 Indian computer experts, and their number grows each year by 10,000; today India is third among the world's countries in this sector, both in quantity and quality. Many Indian computer experts emigrate to the US, especially California, where they are highly sought after. But lately, in order to exploit directly and *in loco* this wealth in human resources, several great computer firms — from Texas Instruments to Hewlett-Packard, from Bull to IBM — have chosen to set up production centers, affiliates, or study centers in India, especially around the city of Bangalore, in the south; it has become the virtual capital of the electronics and computer market. The Bangalore area, like the California area it models itself on, is called Silicon Valley. And

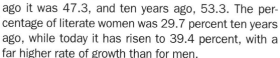

Film posters in Bombay, the capital of commercial movies in India, and in terms of quantity, the most important one in the world.
© Publifoto

India exports software even to the US. Highly sophisticated products thus join the traditional list of Indian exports — cotton textiles, tea, leather, and leather articles. India is also first among the world's countries in diamond-processing (it imports raw diamonds and exports processed ones); 500,000 people are thus employed. Another area in which India can boast world primacy is film production, which is concentrated in Bombay. Each year in India, more films are produced than in any other country in the world, including the US.

Narasimha Rao's government tried to give new stimulus to policies already initiated by Rajiv Gandhi: lessening state control over the economy, partial dismemberment of the public sector, privatization and opening up to foreign capital. Deve Gowda's center-left government, which came to power in May 1996, seemed intent on following this line, even while slowing down reforms for the sake of social welfare, or for greater protection of national industry.

All in all, Indian industry has been strongly stimulated by the changes in recent years, and its growth rate has risen considerably. According to many observers, India stands at the threshold of a true economic boom. One reason for this phenomenon is certainly the low cost of labor. Alongside this factor, we find a vast domestic market, formed by about 200 million members of a bourgeoisie considered "well-to-do." In other words, there should be 200 million people capable of purchasing the consumer goods produced by industry. This market remains to some extent closed with respect to another 336 million Indians, and is completely or almost completely closed to the nearly 314 million living below the poverty line. The enormous gap between haves and have-nots can also be seen by the fact that twenty percent of families make fifty percent of the national income, while another twenty percent receives only five percent.

At the table of the Indian delegation to the General Assembly of the United Nations, in 1960. Nehru sits beside Krishna Menon, a long-time diplomatic and political collaborator.
© Publifoto

Other divergences and strong contrasts appear if we compare different states and geographical areas: the west coast, the south, and the Delhi area attract foreign capital, and in recent years have seen considerable growth, while regions like Bihar, Bengal, and Orissa are still depressed. It is, however, certain that India no longer fits the image of a miserable country, torn by hunger and socio-economic immobility. Though with strong social differences, it is a country on the move.

Ancient and modern problems do continue to hamper India's rhythm of growth, however. They include overpopulation, social and cultural backwardness, and a high foreign debt. Political instability and the uncertainty deriving from ethnic and religious conflict are the heaviest burdens to bear; among other things, they dissuade foreign capitalists from investing in India to the extent that they otherwise might.

Foreign Policy

From its beginning as an independent nation, India has followed a strategy of active neutrality in its foreign policy. Along with Tito, Nasser, Sukharno, and

In recent decades the caste system has been somewhat modified by the advent of modern economic forms, and by the introduction to independent India of a parliamentary regime at least theoretically based on the equality of all citizens. Modern social classes have appeared. Members of the lower castes, or even outcasts, have occasionally managed to obtain economic success and political prestige. However, the caste system continues to play an important role. It has undergone a very limited evolution in the villages (where life has continued to go on according to older rhythms), and a faster one in the cities. Let us take a look at some examples. In India today, agriculture is practiced by ninety percent of the members of farmer castes (the remaining ten percent dedicate themselves to

the fact that agriculture is considered to be a neutral, respectable occupation. Only the members of the highest castes (Brahmins in particular) are reluctant to practice it, because of their aversion to using the hoe, which wounds Mother Earth and the creatures living on her.

The warrior caste has virtually disappeared. The Brahmins (about six percent of the population; the most numerous caste — over fifty percent — is that of the Sudra) are not necessarily priests, although the presence of a Brahmin is always necessary in order to perform the priestly functions. They may be ministers, or entrepreneurs or else servants of a more fortunate Brahmin, or custodians of a poor country temple.

On the other hand, even an untouchable who participates in the political life, and has been

his ministry and goes home, the Brahmin goes back to being Brahmin, and the untouchable, an untouchable. As there is not total identity between a caste and a profession, neither is there total identity between a caste and wealth. There may be rich Sudra farmers and poor Brahmins. However, membership in a caste continues to influence strongly an individual's occupational choices and success. If you meet an intellectual — say, a university professor — he will most probably come from a Brahmin family; if you see a capitalist entrepreneur, he may very easily come from a *jati* of *vaisya*, or merchants. As for untouchables (with few exceptions), if they do not perform their traditional, menial occupations, they are nearly always peasants, sometimes even servants; or else, if they have abandoned their villages in favor of the city, they are manual laborers or members of the working class.

In any case, neither money nor political or cultural renown can cancel out birth. Even in the big cities, where it is no longer always possible for the castes to live in separate neighborhoods, caste solidarity remains strong just the same — though it is less visible. It is well to add that this system, by preventing individuals from freely choosing activities and love relations (or least, by putting obstacles in the way of these choices), has for centuries helped to maintain a relatively rigid society. Even today, it tends to thwart social progress.

other activities); but it is also practiced by forty-three percent of the members of non-agricultural castes. This is due, among other things, to

voted for by many citizens (whether untouchable or not), may be elected as a member of parliament, or appointed minister. But when he leaves

In Indian political life, whether national or local, the electoral success of parties is still strongly linked to support from the most numerous and important castes. Today there still exist in India 110 million outcasts, even though untouchability was officially abolished by the constitution in 1950. The economic conditions of the outcasts, at least in certain regions, have become widely varied, thanks in part to protective legislation and policies (especially with regard to jobs). Nonetheless, being born an outcast is still a curse which brings anxiety and discrimination at work, at home, and in every other aspect of daily life; it even brings recurrent murder threats from Fascist-like groups. In our century, the outcasts have had a great leader: B.R. Ambedkar, who died just a few years ago. Throughout his life, Ambedkar fought to defend the untouchables. In the end, he was so disillusioned that he advocated abandoning Hinduism in favor of mass conversion to Islam or to Buddhism; and tens of thousands heeded this advice. However, even the abandonment of Hinduism sometimes provokes violent reactions. In a number of cases, Hindus of the higher castes have organized and carried out genuine massacres against untouchables, burning down their houses and performing other violent acts. One reason why

Hindus belonging to castes do not favor the untouchables' abandoning Hinduism is a very utilitarian one. Without the untouchables, they would have great difficulty in finding peo-

ple to perform the more impure and degrading occupations, from butchery to burial of the dead. The struggles of the untouchables very often clash with those of the poor peasants (a class to which many untouchables belong). We find the terrible paradox of a highly spiritual religion accompanied by incidents of unprecedented violence. Furthermore, in India, a kind of de facto caste structure exists even among Muslims and Christians, though it is less rigid. In Bengal there are mosques where untouchables who have converted to Islam are forbidden to enter, and in many Christian churches of southern India, the untouch-

ables stay well away from members of the higher castes during the liturgical functions. This ancient system is so profoundly rooted in the Indian consciousness that it is, at present, difficult to foresee its end, in spite of the attacks that are made against it by the process of modernization. The outcasts are not the only "pariahs" of Indian society. In India today there are still about sixty million *adivasi* or original inhabitants who live in frequently primitive conditions in the mountainous regions of the north or in the forests of the interior. Among the *adivasi* there are ancient peoples of Australoid stock (for example, the Munda of central India, and the Vedda of the island of Sri Lanka) but also simple linguistic minorities: Tibeto-Burman (Tibetans, Tripuri, Naga, Mizo), proto-Dravidic or Aryo-Dravidic (Bhil, Gond, Santal), and others. These peoples are sometimes designated as "tribal," or "classified castes," and are the beneficiaries of protective legal norms. But they are also subjected to strong pressure to assimilate (which they try to resist). And often, they are victims of abuse. ■

Left, untouchables in prayer during Gandhi's fast on their behalf, 1932. Above, a barber in Benares. The jati of barbers usually belong to the fourth caste (varna), that of the sudra.

New Delhi, 1959; demonstrators against repression in Tibet, in front of the Chinese embassy.
© Publifoto

Zhou Enlai, Nehru was one of the most important leaders of the non-aligned Afro-Asiatic countries which united at Bandung in 1955. India maintained cordial relations with the Soviet Union and with countries in the Communist bloc. The India Premier also attempted to sustain friendly relations with China, but he soon came up against the obstacle represented by China's border claims in Ladakh and in the Himalayas. Beijing, unlike New Delhi, had never accepted the dividing line between India and Tibet (the "MacMahon line") drawn on a map by the British in 1914. Border incidents broke out as early as 1956–1957, and the crisis between the two countries worsened further after China's armed repression of the Tibet rebellion (1959), and the Dalai Lama's flight to India, along with many of his followers.

Armed battles broke out in 1959–1960. In 1962, they were followed by a full-scale attack by the Chinese army, which was able to exploit the element of surprise. When, hardly more than a month later, the Chinese unilaterally declared a ceasefire, a vast area had come under their control. Beijing withdrew its armed forces from nearly all the Indian territory it had conquered, but kept part of Ladakh, as well as the strategically important border regions in the high Himalayas. The Indian government had to make the best of things, and accept the de facto consequences of a military defeat which cost Nehru's popularity a great deal. The premier was harshly criticized for the lack of training demonstrated by the Indian army.

The war between India and China had not been caused only by the perennial border disputes or by the fate of Tibet, but also by complex political motives. The Chinese intended to declare their prestige and supremacy in the Third World, in the face of any potential competitor. They also intended to create difficulties for the Indian model of democratic and capitalistic development, which at the time was often proposed in contrast to the Chinese collectivistic, authoritarian one. Finally, they wanted to challenge the Soviet Union itself, whose policy of détente they had been opposing for years.

During the years which followed, India turned to the US and Great Britain for military aid (though aid was generally limited). More importantly, it further developed its cordial relations with the Soviet Union, both in economic and military areas. Especially after American intervention in Vietnam, which the Indian gov-

Indian infantry marching towards Dacca during the 1971 war with Pakistan. On that occasion India supported the secession of East Pakistan (Bangladesh).

Indian artillery posts on the Himalayan glacier of Siachen. Since 1984 India and Pakistan have been confronting each other continuously on the "rooftop of the world."
© 2 Publifoto

ernment strongly criticized, Indian "socialism" came progressively nearer and nearer to Soviet positions in foreign policy. This choice made it more and more difficult to believe the government's persistent official declarations of "active neutrality" and "non-alignment." Little by little, there grew up an Indian-Soviet axis in opposition to a US-Pakistan-China axis. Only after the death of Indira Gandhi, and particularly after the dissolution of the Soviet Union, did this privileged relationship loosen. Indian diplomacy has had to look for a new, balanced position, by developing contacts and relations both with the West — including the US — and eastern Asia. And India has always tried to affirm its strategic political leadership by prudently and gradually claiming a powerful regional role, both on the subcontinent and over the whole of the Indian Ocean.

Ever since its birth as an independent nation, India has fought a number of wars, nearly always border disputes: twice with China (in 1959–1960 and in 1962), and three times with Pakistan (in 1947–1949, in 1965, and in 1971). In 1965, the Indian army was compensated for its defeat three years before at the hands of the Chinese, by victoriously resisting an attack by Pakistan. That conflict ended the following year at Tashkent, with a treaty painstakingly reached by Shastri, Nehru's successor; the Soviets served as mediators. In 1971, India interceded in support of a rebellion in East Pakistan (later named Bangladesh), playing an important role in its success.

In the mid 1970s, India annexed what became its twenty-second state, the small Himalayan kingdom of Sikkim. Another small kingdom, Bhutan, the larger Nepal, and Bangladesh itself (which was extremely poor, and surrounded by Indian territory on every side), did what they could to defend themselves against the attentions of their powerful neighbor, which considered them to be protectorates. In 1988, Indian intervention in the Maldives saved a regime which was direly threat-

ened by the invasion of Tamil mercenaries from Sri Lanka. Finally, Rajiv Gandhi sent a strong military contingent into nearby Sri Lanka, with the task of remaining long enough to pacify the zone; but he was then forced to withdraw and acknowledge failure. India, at any rate, is considered the fourth military power in the world, after the US, Russia, and China; it has the atom bomb at its disposal (the first nuclear explosion, greeted with great enthusiasm, occurred in 1974, in the underground of the Rajasthan desert). Relations with Pakistan remain tense; indeed, they have worsened since 1990, especially because of the Kashmir problem. In Kashmir, the two national armies have been shooting at each other with cannons for years, with tiring regularity, among the highest peaks in the world. Nor are India's relations with China particularly cordial (though there have been improvements), given their persistent border disputes, and the hospitality offered by India to Tibetans struggling for independence.

Chapter 5

GANDHI'S LEGACY: A SUMMING UP

A SUBJECT OF DEBATE FOR SOME, YET UNIVERSALLY RESPECTED BEYOND ANY EFFORTS TO SANCTIFY HIM, GANDHI REMAINS ONE OF THE GREAT FIGURES (AND THE FEW POSITIVE ONES) OF A CENTURY THAT HAS KNOWN HORROR AND GENOCIDE OF EVERY SORT. TODAY HIS POLITICAL AND CULTURAL LEGACY BELONGS TO ALL OF US.

A medieval-style hagiography exists for the Mahatma. Gandhi is seen as a saintly man, a generous Utopian — though a trifle bizarre. According to this point of view, it was his saintliness that enabled him to touch the religious heart of his people in order to unify it and lead it to victory over the British. In contrast to this view, some recent historians have insisted on the figure of Gandhi as a politician, trained in the tactics of power, as was demonstrated by the way he won control of the Congress Party in the years immediately following World War I.

When asked the "saint-or-politician?" question in 1920, Gandhi wrote an article declaring he was neither. The concept of sanctity seemed to him too elevated and sacred to be applied to a man living on this earth, who must daily face earthly problems: "a humble seeker of truth, who knows his limits, makes mistakes, and never hesitates to admit it when he makes them." But Gandhi also denied being a politician in the traditional sense of the word. He was, he said, a politician trying to introduce religion to politics. What religion? Gandhi's, naturally: the search for Truth. He was, to put it briefly, a politician who changed the rules of the game: who refused to endorse, for example, the idea that the end justifies the means.

Gandhi's memory is entrusted to monuments, and to the Indian collective consciousness. But independent India has chosen different paths from those he proposed.
© Publifoto

"The means," he wrote in 1909, "can be compared to a seed, the end to a tree." Between the means and the end there is the same inviolable relation that exists between the seed and the tree. We reap "exactly what we sow." Gandhi always used extreme clarity in conducting and explaining his political philosophy and actions. He always maintained an attitude of clarity and loyalty, combined with firmness, even with respect to the British.

An improvised meeting at a train stop.

But Gandhi also had an acute sense of organization, and was capable of practicing politics in a more traditional sense. A British viceroy who had occasion to deal with him noted that he may have been a saint and a prophet, but that he was the "shrewdest little man," and the cleverest negotiator that he had ever known; the one gifted with the subtlest political sense. At times, Gandhi "practiced politics" when this seemed necessary to built the foundation for the type of action that he most cared about; but this practice was never such that it made him pay too high a price — a price that could not be justified in the light of his ethics. More than once, when he thought that this ethical line was about to be crossed, he withdrew from political posts of responsibility in order to close himself into his ashram, or journey from one Indian village to another, spreading his ideas. Globally speaking, in his Indian activities, from 1915 till his death, Gandhi was much more rarely a political leader in the strictest sense than a sort of great adviser to Congress (with which he sometimes came into conflict); and an imaginative, charismatic popular leader, capable of inventing unpredictable initiatives at the right moment.

A man of rare moral consistency, Gandhi was at the

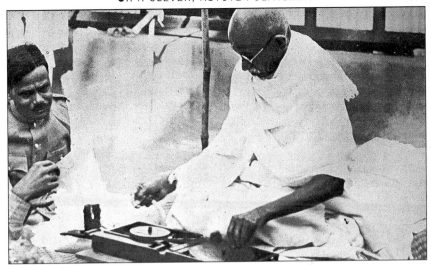

same time against what he called the "fetish of consistency." In his search for the Truth, he said, he had abandoned many ideas and learned many new things. As old as he was, he never felt that he had stopped growing in spirit. What he cared about was his readiness to heed the call of Truth — his "God" — from moment to moment.

Gandhi's autobiography contains an episode that reveals him to be a bit less rigorous than usual (a bit less of a "saint"), and which helps to free him from the confines of hagiography. In 1912, he had made a vow to abstain from drinking milk, out of compliance with his purely vegetarian diet. A few years later he fell seriously ill, and the doctors were unable to cure him, especially because of his dietary limitations. Gandhi longed to be cured in order to take up a *satyagrahi* campaign that he cared deeply about. On a suggestion from his wife, Kasturbai, he became persuaded that his vow concerned cow and buffalo milk, but not goat's milk. So thanks to goat's milk, he got better. He later suffered from feelings of guilt over what he considered a betrayal of his principles. But meanwhile, he was cured.

Gandhi dedicated a certain number of hours each day to spinning cotton, while simultaneously performing other activities. The moment referred to in this photo is particularly dramatic: a police officer is informing him of the situation in the district of Noakhali, in West Bengal. There, in the autumn of 1946, Muslims perpetrated horrible massacres against Hindus; this started a series of riots between the two communities throughout the country. The elderly Gandhi visited Noakhali, putting his life in danger while journeying up and down the district on a desperate pilgrimage for peace.

Gandhi's Concept of Non-violence

Underlying Gandhi's concept of non-violence was an ethical belief. Gandhi was highly influenced by ten-

Gandhi offers a glass of water to a Muslim woman fasting for the sake of unity between Hindus and Muslims.

dencies long present in Indian thought (in Hinduism, in Jainism) which condemned not only killing, but hurting, harming, or inflicting suffering on any human being — indeed, any living being. But he was also influenced by scripture from other religions, such as the Gospels: the Sermon on the Mount had deeply struck him by its exhortation to love one's enemy, and to react to offense by turning the other cheek.

This ethical conviction was strengthened by his experience. Gandhi was not an organic or systematic thinker. He entitled his autobiography *The Story of my Experiments with Truth*. And on many occasions in the course of his lifetime, he chose to insist on this important role of experiment. In 1936, he wrote: "The opinions I have formed and the conclusions I have reached are not definite. I could modify them at any moment." In Gandhi's thought, then, ethical principles went hand in hand with the observation of historical facts: for example, direct knowledge of violence, which he came to meet more than once.

In any case, Gandhi's *satyagraha* must not be thought of as a doctrine of resignation. Gandhi intended to modify the world, not accept it. He intended to oppose evil actively in order to defeat it. He intended to combat injustice. He did not deny conflict, but only the use of violence to resolve it.

Gandhi had many good reasons to refuse violence. Violence, he maintained, never leads to a lasting or stable solution to conflict. Using violence tends to generate further violence, and brutalize both sides. It tends to bring forth authoritarian men, who continue to exercise violence once victory has been reached. Moreover, it implies secrecy and suspicion, falsity, unilateral action, and excessive simplification of truth. In so doing, it perpetuates an old culture and mentality, instead of favoring the development of a better type of person — one more sincere, serene, altruistic, unselfish, free, and tolerant.

Gandhi also refused that limited, tactical kind of non-violence which he called non-violence of the weak. That is, he refused recourse to non-violence exclusively as an opportunistic choice, made by those who are unable to fight with other means, since they would other-

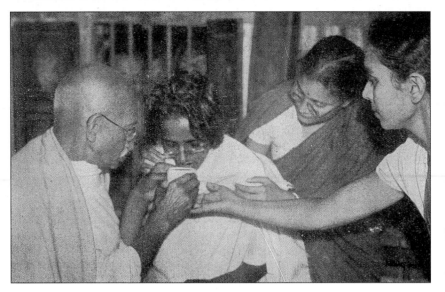

Upon his return to India after his studies in London, Gandhi defined himself as a "reformer" — that is, an admirer and follower of figures who had in various ways tried to reform and modernize Hinduism: Ram Mohan Roy, Debendranath Tagore, Dayananda Sarasvati. He probably appreciated in them (as he did in the *Bhagavad Gita*) the vigorous exhortation to action in the world, as against an Indian tradition that had favored, instead, evasion from the world.

As early as 1894, judging from a letter written by Raychandbhai, he was immersed in a religious search: a very intense one, but full of uncertainties. Later he became more sure in his adherence to Hinduism, the religion of his fathers, while favoring its ethical and social aspects over the metaphysical ones, and welcoming influence from other faiths. He synthesized his conception of Hinduism by saying that the way to attaining *moksha* (i.e., "freeing oneself from the evil cycle of births and deaths and immersing oneself in Brahma") is to do pure and good acts, have compassion for every living being, and live in truth. Gandhi also saw Hinduism as a synthesis of Indian religious experiences, and considered Jainism and Buddhism as part of these experiences.

In spite of his personal preference for a faith reduced to a few essential elements, he had a deep respect for the various forms of popular worship. He thought that all religions were branches of the same tree, that each of them contained a nucleus of truth, and that every religion had performed a role necessary to "the people to whom it had been revealed."

He was therefore opposed to conversions: each person must practice in the best way possible the religion into which he or she has been born and educated. Consistent with this vision of the religious phenomenon, he was an advocate of total separation between religions and the State. The State, he said, had nothing to do with religion. The State should occupy itself with our worldly welfare, health, communications, foreign policy, currency, and so forth; but "not with your and my religion." That is a matter involving each one of us personally. ■

wise be defeated. He refused a merely defensive concept of non-violence used in order to limit losses in the face of an oppressor, a stronger enemy. For this reason, as years went by, he used the expression "passive resistance" less and less. In Gandhi's opinion, non-violence was supposed to become a weapon for the courageous, not a shield for cowards. On more than one occasion, he went so far as to say that violence seemed preferable to a cowardly, resigned acceptance of injustice. Gandhi's non-violence, then, was a weapon of attack, meant to defeat and convert the enemy by forcing him to face

"No-one can be actively non-violent and not rebel against injustice, wherever it may be found."

another's determination to fight and suffer.

True *satyagrahi*, the true non-violent combatants, will fight not only for their own sake, but also for that of their enemies. They will respect their enemies; they will try to understand their motives (because there are many truths) and they will abstain from any form of struggle meant to destroy them or inflict suffering beyond the loss of their unjust privileges. One must fight in order to re-establish truth and justice, not to create new injustice or seek revenge capable of generating new violence. Gandhi led his struggles with incredible loyalty. He never adopted a strategy of surprise: before undertaking an initiative, he always informed his adversary.

If many truths exist, and if the enemy is not to be destroyed, the solution to any conflict is compromise. Gandhi's legacy contains beautiful examples of this idea. After defending his first important case in court, he observed that a lawyer's most important function is to reunite the disagreeing parties. In his autobiography, again, he wrote that his passion for truth had taught him the "beauty of compromise." And to his biographer, Louis Fischer, he said: "I am essentially a man inclined to compromise because I am never sure

of possessing the truth." Even so, it must be added, he declared numerous times that compromise must never prevail over principles, nor must it ever imply mere tactics.

"Once, when people wanted to fight, they measured their own physical strength; today, a single man with a firearm can, from a hillside, take the life of thousands. This is civilization."

(Hind Swaraj, 1909)

Are "Exceptions" Admissible?

Like Tolstoy, the other great "holistic pacifist," Gandhi admitted the existence of exceptional situations in which non-violence was not practicable. In Tolstoy's view, Christ forbade men to oppose an evil person, or to commit violence in any case, except to save a child in danger. As for Gandhi, in an article of 1926,

Gandhi's figure and his ideas are widespread in contemporary Indian fiction written in English. We shall mention here three examples:

Waiting for the Mahatma is the title of a novel by R.K. Narayan. In *Untouchable*, by Mulk Raj Anand, the concluding scene begins with a crowd shouting that the Mahatma has arrived. But the presence — including the physical presence — of Gandhi among the protagonists is virtually the only characteristic uniting these two novels and their authors. The novelists are the same age, equally long-lived, and are both among the most respected writers in Anglo-Indian literature. But they are vastly different from one another.

Born in Peshawar (now in Pakistan) in 1905, Anand studied in London and Cambridge, and began his writing career in England: it was E.M. Forster who wrote the preface to *Untouchable* in 1935. For many years Anand was a true "westernized oriental gentleman," and a left-leaning intellectual; he even went to Spain during the civil war. In England he wrote the first version of the novel, then went to visit Gandhi at his ashram in Sabarmati, so that the Mahatma could read it. He remained there for three months, after agreeing to put aside his British gentleman's clothing and wear simpler, traditional garb; promising chastity and sobriety, at least temporarily; and promising to clean the latrines once a week. In recompense, Gandhi virtually made him rewrite

the novel, forcing him to use a simpler, more realistic style, free of literary conceits. Although *Untouchable* is a novel and not a political or sociological essay, Anand uses the novel form in order to describe and denounce the intolerable condition of that category of Indians variously known as untouchables, pariahs, or, more correctly, outcasts. *Untouchable* is the story of a day in the life of a young outcast, a street-sweeper and son of street-sweepers, whose task is to clean the public toilets. In a way it is a day like all the rest, made up of the tasks, experiences, and humiliations which are a normal part of the protagonist's life. But the sweet, sensitive young man of the first pages, capable of attenuating his harsh condition through an ingenious inclination to fantasy, is thrown into crisis during the course of his day; he feels a painful anxiety grow within him. He happens to end up in a crowd awaiting the arrival of the Mahatma, and listens to his speech. When Gandhi says he considers untouchability to be "the most shameful stain on Hinduism," the young man is won over. Other opinions, overheard in the little groups clustered about after the meeting is over, complicate his ideas. But this does not prevent him from going home at the end of the day with a new awareness of his condition, and of his possible future. We can very well say that Anand projected his own uncertainties onto the characters, leaving them unresolved

at the end of the novel. Anand admired in Gandhi the love of truth and equality of men, and the method of non-violence. At the same time, he was a progressive, and this distanced him from Gandhi's criticism of modern technological civilization.

Unlike Anand, a strongly social and populist narrator (and a bit of a preacher), R.K. Narayan, born in Madras in 1907, was throughout his life a supporter of the autonomy of literature: an adversary of the excessive intrusion of politics into artistic creation. His *Waiting for the Mahatma* was written in 1955. Narayan did not share all of Gandhi's ideas, but he nurtured respect and sympathy for the man and for his love of truth. He often introduced "Gandhian" characters into his novels. In *Waiting for the Mahatma*, there is something more: as in *Untouchable*, Gandhi appears in person. But Narayan's distance from Anand is immediately apparent. Here, the Mahatma appears much more frequently than in Anand's book, but in a less solemn, more intimate and joyful context. The narrative highlights an event combining love and politics, and giving definite precedence to the former, as it involves the behavior and anxiety of the main character, a lazy, twenty year old dreamer living in Malgudi, the imaginary city in southern India which forms the setting of all Narayan's novels. The young man meets a god-daughter of Gandhi, and falls in love with her. When the Mahatma arrives in Malgudi to give a speech, he promises Gandhi he will change his lifestyle, and consecrate himself to driving the British out of India. In reality, his conversion is rather superficial. The girl persuades him that militancy must take precedence over personal sentiment; they must wait. When the two separate (she turns herself in to a British prison, in 1942; while he carries on the fight from outside), the young man lets himself be brainwashed by a follower of Chandra Bose, and dedicates himself to minor acts of terrorism. In the end, however, a few years later, Gandhi pardons him for these experiences, and also blesses the union of the two young people. Immediately afterward, the Mahatma is assassinated. In spite of this dramatic ending, in which the author seems to render somber homage to the field of History and to one of its heroes, the predominate tone of the novel, as always in Narayan, is ironic. And the center of attention remains the day-to-day events in the lives of common people, who are often overwhelmed by chance and by forces more powerful than they are, spinning out of their control. The novel contains pages in which this irony, ever animated by solidarity and compassion, turns to high comedy: as in the scene where Gandhi, having arrived in Malgudi, chooses to live in

a street-sweeper's hut, causing disappointment and frustration among the notables of the city who have prepared a much more luxurious, even regal, kind of hospitality. The street-sweeper, then, reappears here, and here, too, Gandhi speaks about untouch-

ability — but in a very different context. In Narayan, the character's relationship with the evils of the world is more calm and indirect.

Published in 1938, *Kanthapura*, by Raja Rao (born in the state of Mysore in 1909) tells of how Gandhi's message is received and transformed into action in a poor village of southern India. It also shows (even more explicitly than in the two above-mentioned novels) the difficulties and contradictions of this action's devel-

opment. The claim to national independence, the dissemination of hand-spinning, the battle against untouchability and against the inferiority of women clash not only with the more obvious adversaries of each kind of change, but also with the burdens of tradition, ignorance, inertia, and ancient orthodoxies. Later, the inhabitants of the village who find themselves facing harsh repression gradually start to doubt the efficacy of non-violence. The doubt is expressed in the admiration of some for the greater social radicalism found in Nehru, or in the communist militants. But all this does not prevent Gandhi's message from being affirmed and translated into action with extraordinary courage, until the village is defeated and destroyed by the police. Gandhi never appears here in person, but the whole novel is dominated by his silent presence. His ideas are here, as are his followers. When the villagers of Kanthapura are won over, they see in the Mahatma a reincarnation of the god-hero Rama, in his battle waged against the evil Ravan in order to free his beloved wife, Sita. The novel thus combines contemporary history (the year is 1930) and ancient myths. The author turns over the task of reconciling these two temporal elements to a narrator who is a wise Brahman widow. ∎

he formulated the hypothesis of a mad murderer who threatens a community: "In some cases it may even be necessary to shed human blood," he wrote. Suppose a man were seized by homicidal madness and started running around with a sword in his hand, killing anyone in his path, and no one had the courage to capture him alive. Whoever killed the madman would gain the gratitude of the community, and be considered a charitable man. According to *ahimsa*, in fact, it is the clear duty of every person to kill such a man. There is an exception, if one would call it that. The *yogi* who is capable of placating the fury of such a man may refrain from killing him. But normal men have not reached this perfection; the question supposes a society of normal mortal beings. A person who does not kill a murderer threatening to kill his child (when he cannot prevent murder in any other way) has no merit, but commits a sin: "he is not practicing *ahimsa*, but *himsa*" (violence), through an erroneous conception of *ahimsa*.

One may well see a wider, symbolic meaning in this hypothesis proposed by Gandhi. One can see the madman threatening the village as an allegorical figure of Hitler, threatening the world community. Certainly, even from the point of view of non-violence, there is nothing worse than standing by indifferently to watch a massacre, or turning the theory of non-violence into an alibi for selfishness and indifference.

However, as the Second World War approached, and during its early phase, Gandhi assumed "scandalous" positions (or at least, some considered them to be such). He advised Czechs, Poles, and Jews to oppose the Nazis with the mere force of non-violence. In 1940, he appreciated the "courage" of French statesmen (the men of Vichy) who had "accepted the inevitable by refusing to become accomplices to an absurd massacre." He asked the British to abandon the struggle, to lay down their arms and serenely accept the fate that Hitler had reserved for them. He even wrote to Hitler. Even while considering Hitlerism the "elevation of brute force to the rank of exact science to be applied with scientific precision," he did not give up hope that Hitler himself might "become sensitive to human suffering." For a long time he continued to believe that even dictators could be converted.

It has been observed that geographical and cultural distance prevented Gandhi from understanding the nature of modern totalitarianism. He compared the position of Czechs, Poles, and Jews with respect to the Nazis to that of Indians with respect to the British. He did not understand that Nazism had gone beyond the confines of any possibility for non-violent confrontation, except at the price of genocide. It is true that Gandhi saw and forcefully condemned the barbarizing effects of the war, which he witnessed with great anguish. Still, his attitude toward Nazism also showed the contradictions present in any kind of radical and holistic pacifism. (It would be intriguing to compare it with the tormented attitude of such a great European personality as Simone Weil, who was convinced, on the eve of the Second World War, that any tragedy, even the threat of German hegemony, was preferable to war; and then resolved, once the conflict had begun, "after a painful interior struggle," to "pursue the destruction of Hitler with or without hope for success.")

In a way, the Gandhi of 1939–1941 seems to demand an impossible heroism from those "common mortal beings" (not, then, quasi-perfect men) of whom he had spoken in the article of 1926: as if now he were

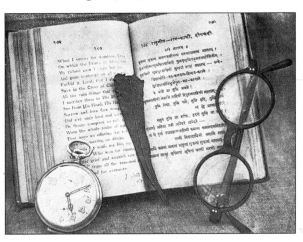

*A*bove, objects belonging to Gandhi and, left, the last letter written by the Mahatma, dated January 29, 1948.

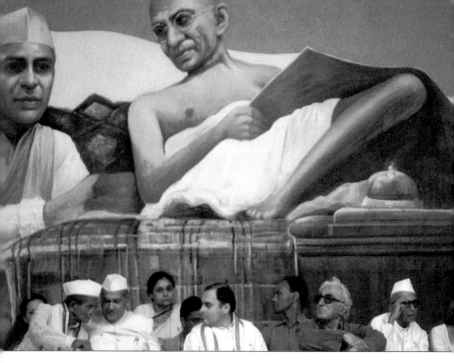

The image of Gandhi, "Father of the homeland," set beside that of Nehru, in a mural behind Rajiv Gandhi, the son of Indira.

driven by impatience, by a will to make up for lost time, even at the cost of sacrificing an entire generation in the name of a future capacity for peaceful relations among men.

Holistic pacifism, in fact, finds one of its main contradictions in the matter of "wars of defense": an ambiguous category, certainly, but not easy to shunt aside. How is it possible not to react to evil when it manifests itself in the harm of the innocent, beside us and before our very eyes? How can we condemn a person who defends himself from abuse, a people (but also a government having a regular army, together with those who aid it) who resists foreign invasion? To oppose any type of violence *a priori*, even when defensive, in a world still dominated by violence, risks making us accomplices in aggression, massacres, genocide. (Such forms of complicity have appeared more than once.) What's more, radical pacifism tends to close its eyes to the problem of freedom or — and this amounts to the same thing — to the question of what makes life in a peaceful world worth living. These remain open questions, impossible to ignore.

Gandhi's Legacy in Independent India

In independent India, Gandhi was simultaneously beatified and forgotten.

The political choices of Nehru and other leaders of the new state were in many respects quite different from those envisioned and preached by Gandhi (let it suffice to mention centralism, a planned economy, and the primacy of heavy industry). Hardly any of his ideas regarding India's development were adopted. Gandhi's legacy was thus reduced to a few volunteer experiments, significant but limited, such as the Bhudan Yajna ("Gift of Earth") movement created in 1951 by a disciple of the Mahatma, Acharya Vinoba Bhave (1895–1982). Accompanied by his disciples, Vinoba set out on foot to journey around the countryside in order to convince landowners to give their poorest peasants part of their lands. The government favored the experiment, viewing it as an alternative to the peasant demonstrations organized by the communists; the results, however, were modest in scope. Jayaprakash Narayan (1902–1979) participated in the Bhudan movement as well, and later took up some of the goals and methods of Gandhi in opposition to Indira Gandhi.

The Mahatma in a caricature drawn in 1932 by Elsa King.

In compensation for this ideological neglect, there is no protagonist of India's modern history in whose honor more monuments have been built than Gandhi (Subhas Chandra Bose, the man who symbolized the choice of armed struggle against the British, comes in second). The Mahatma's houses and ashrams are visited with devotion, as are the numerous museums dedicated to him. There are foundations fostering the study and dissemination of his thought, and others inspired by it to pursue humanitarian or pacifist causes.

Groups of Gandhians also head small rural communities, schools, and clinics. An institution founded by Gandhi himself, the Navajivan Trust, holds the copyrights to all of the Mahatma's writings, and publishes them itself. A national edition of Gandhi's complete works has been published since 1956 in over ninety volumes, both in English and in Hindi, under the auspices of a special department of the Ministry of Information. Finally, a journal, *Gandhi Marg*, is dedicated to Gandhi studies (*marg* means "path").

Like narrative fiction, the cinema, too, has been interested in Gandhi, though its offerings have not been as fine. Its most famous produce is *Gandhi*, directed by the Englishman, Richard Attenborough in 1982, and awarded eight Oscars; a grand film in "colossal" style, rich with an epic and pedagogical tone, it required twenty years of work and the active collaboration of the Indian government. Much of the film's interest lies in the high skill of the actors (starting with Ben Kingsley as Gandhi), who studied for a long time and with great precision the attitudes, gestures, even the tics, of their respective characters, using photographic and cinematic documentary material. Nevertheless, it gives a slightly idealized picture, tending to brush over contradictions, and often limiting itself to rather superficial explanations of the Mahatma's acts. This has not prevented it from performing a great role in the rebirth of worldwide interest in this protagonist of twentieth-century history.

Nearly twenty years before Attenborough's film, in 1963, *Nine Hours to Rama* was produced by the American director, Mark Robson. Its main theme, narrated with a certain amount of suspense, was the assassination of the Mahatma, and the conspiracy leading up to it. Gandhi was played by Harry Andrews. In other Hollywood films, Gandhi or his followers remain in the background. This is the case for *Bhowani Junction*, directed by

George Cukor in 1956 — a full-blown sentimental drama in which Ava Gardner and Stewart Granger get romantically involved while the Indians are massacring each other and the British; and also for *Thunder in the Dust* directed by Charles Vidor, in which Charles Boyer plays the role of a "Gandhian" minister employed by a maharaja assassinated by rebels. After appearing as a kind, peaceful man throughout most of the film (albeit a bit fanatical and extravagant), in the end he can stand it no longer and starts shooting furiously. (The moral is that nonviolence does not pay.)

Other films are useful in recreating the atmosphere of India at the time of British rule, or immediately following it: above all, the films of the great Indian director Satyajit Ray (*Panther Panchali, Aparajito, Apur Sansar*) and James Ivory's many refined films set in India; *The River*, by Renoir; Rossellini's *India*; Lang's *Indian Tomb*; Malle's *Calcutta*; and David Lean's *A Passage to India*. Like the two films mentioned by Cukor and Vidor, *Life of a Bengal Lancer* by Hathaway, *Rains of Ranchipur* by Brown, *Gunga Din* by Stevens and *Kim*, by Saville, belong to the category of purely commercial films. Still they have a certain documentary value. If nothing else, they are important in helping us to reconstruct the West's (or, if you will, Hollywood's) image of India. ■

Ben Kingsley in Gandhi, *Richard Attenborough's 1982 film.*

Gandhi's memory is kept alive with official ritual by the government. Which, having renounced his ideas, still makes an effort to manage their legacy in the form of propaganda. Even Richard Attenborough's film was approved by Nehru, who wanted to take credit for his connection to the Gandhi legacy. All this may be disappointing from one point of view; however, it does bear witness to a deep memory left in India's collective consciousness.

Fame and Influence of Gandhi in the World

Some have considered Gandhi an "Eastern thinker" like many others, a noble and extravagant figure, depository of an ancient wisdom that can be enjoyably consumed in bite-size pieces from an elegant, accurate collection of thoughts on religion, tolerance, the destiny of man, and so forth. A corollary of this interpretation lies in the act of removing the man and his works: in confining him to a typically Indian environment, not relevant elsewhere.

The truth of the matter is that many facts contradict each of these interpretations. In the first place, Gandhi was not only a "thinker," but a great political leader, who competed with what was (though it would not be for long) the greatest empire in the world. In the second place, Gandhi's entire cultural formation contradicts that idea of a total separation, or "otherness," between East and West. Once, during one of his stays in London, Gandhi gave a speech on East and West, in which he refuted the first line of Kipling's famous poem: "*Oh, East is East and West is West, and never the twain shall meet.*" He said he agreed, instead, with Tennyson, who in his *Vision* had foreseen, in the figure of a prophet, a union of the two civilizations. One might add that in Kipling's poem itself, if we go beyond the first line (which is nearly always quoted alone), the vision becomes surprisingly more complex: *Oh, East is East and West is West, and never the twain shall meet, / Till Earth and Sky stand presently at God's great Judgment Seat; / But there is neither East nor West, Border, nor Breed, nor Birth, / When two strong men stand face to face, though they come from the ends of the earth!*

"*Truth and* ahimsa *will never be destroyed, but if Gandhism is another name for sectarianism, it deserves to be destroyed. If I were to know, after my death, that what I stood for had degenerated into sectarianism, I should be deeply pained. We have to work away silently. Let no one say that he is a follower of Gandhi. It is enough that I should be my own follower. I know what an inadequate follower I am of myself, for I cannot live up to the convictions I stand for.*"

Harijan, March 1940

The demonstrations for democracy in China in the spring of 1989 and dramatically concluded by the armed repression of early June, also marked the entrance of nonviolence into the political panorama of China. This image is taken from a brief televised scene that was seen all over the world and became a symbol of Tienanmen Square and the heroism of the individual who single-handedly offers himself up to the armed violence of an authoritarian state structure.

Finally, Gandhi has had followers and imitators in many parts of the world. Just think of the passive resistance adopted by many Norwegians (especially teachers) against the Nazi occupation; of the battles of African Americans led by Martin Luther King, Jr.; of the Solidarity movement in Poland; of the overthrow of Ferdinand Marcos in the Philippines; of the young people involved in the "Beijing Spring" of 1989; of the nonviolent position of the Dalai Lama, Tensi Gyatso, leader of the Tibetan people's struggle; of the extraordinarily courageous resistance against the Burmese military dictatorship, conducted by a woman, Aung San Suu Kyi. All these cases have involved examples of "effective" struggle, although (for the moment) not all of them have brought victory. By itself or in cooperation with other currents of thought, Gandhi's influence has been and still is strong, in guiding anti-war movements, struggles of conscientious objectors, and other civil rights battles, studies on peace research and non-violent

defense, and various individual and collective life choices.

In recent times, a rediscovery of Gandhi (symbolized, we might say, by the world-wide success of Attenborough's film) has been linked to great pacifist movements, and to the increasingly widespread interest in nature, ecology, animal rights, nutrition and body hygiene (themes dear to Gandhi, long before they became popular).

"Organized pacifism" has been the object of much criticism, from many sides. We can divide the objections into two groups. On one hand, many pacifist movements (e.g., the "partisans for peace" during the Cold War era) have been criticized for becoming instruments of propaganda — usually, pro-Soviet ones, but at any rate, anti-Western. On the other hand, it has been possible to perceive the discomfort of those same movements when, after the fall of the Berlin Wall (and with it, the end of the division of the world into two oppos-

One could see a young man stopping a column of tanks. The commander of the column, taken by surprise, shifted direction in order to avoid hitting the young man, but the latter shifted in turn, climbed up onto the tank and started speaking to its occupants. The young man's name was Wang Weilin. It seems he was arrested and killed near the site, shortly after this episode.

ing blocs), world politics became more complicated. It suddenly became impossible, or nearly so, to effect a Manichean separation between the good and the evil, between friends and enemies. On more than one occasion, pacifism was accused of having reached a state of virtual paralysis. It seemed incapable of intervening in any positive sense; indeed, it even seemed to thwart international action meant to stop or discourage local wars and brutal massacres.

Many people argue that pacifism often shows a unilateral, simplistic nature, tending to underestimate problems like that of freedom or tyranny. These are — nearly all of them — problems that Gandhi faced. Even today, we can draw from his thought and experience to enrich our current debates.

Orwell's Opinion

The author of *Animal Farm* and *1984* was born to an English family living in India, and he later served in the Burma police force. During World War II he worked for the BBC in preparing programs directed at an Indian audience, in order to counter Axis propaganda. These were three good reasons for his interest in Indian matters. Orwell was both fascinated and repelled by the figure of Gandhi. He was highly critical of him in some ways. For example, he did not share his excessive zeal in exhorting men to virtue, and in some way claimed the right to "nonsanctity," since it is part of man's essential nature never to reach perfection.

Orwell wrote an essay on Gandhi in 1948, shortly after the Mahatma's death. In the concluding page, he admitted he had never felt much liking for Gandhi, but conceded his admiration for the man as political thinker; Gandhi had not been "wrong in the main," nor had his life been a "failure." His main political objective, "the peaceful ending of British rule, had after all been attained." Though Orwell points out that it was the Labour Government that pulled out of India, and that a Conservative Government, especially under Churchill would have behaved differently, still it was indisputable that a vast wave of public opinion had developed in Britain which favored Indian independence. He wondered how much of this was due to Gandhi's personal influence. If Britain and India were one day to establish honest and friendly relations, would it be partly because "Gandhi, by keeping up his struggle obstinately and without hatred, disinfected the political air?" (The very fact that one should ask such questions, said Orwell, revealed the stature of the man.)

One can feel, wrote Orwell, "as I do, a sort of aesthetic disgust for Gandhi, one can reject the claims of sainthood made on his behalf (he never made any such claim himself by the way), one may also reject sainthood as an ideal and therefore feel that Gandhi's basic aims were anti-human and reactionary: but regarded simply as a politician, and compared with the leading political figures of our time, how clean a smell he has managed to leave behind!"

Bibliography

Introductory works:

■ Johnson, G., *A Cultural Atlas of India.* New York: Facts on File, 1996.

■ Robinson, F. (Ed.), *Cambridge Encyclopedia of India, Pakistan, Bangladesh, Sri Lanka, Nepal, Bhutan and the Maldives.* Cambridge: Cambridge University Press, 1989.

General history:

■ *Cambridge History of India.* 5 vols. Cambridge: Cambridge University Press, 1922–1937.

■ *Cambridge Economic History of India.* 2 vols. Cambridge: Cambridge University Press, 1980–1983.

■ Brown, J.M., *Modern India: The Origins of an Asian Democracy.* Oxford: Oxford University Press, 1985.

■ Guha, R., ed., *Subaltern Studies.* 8 vols. New Delhi: Oxford University Press, 1982–95.

■ Majumdar, R.C., *History of the Freedom Movement in India.* 3 vols. Calcutta: Mukhopadhyay, 1971–1977.

■ Nehru, J., *The Discovery of India.* London: Meridian Press, 1956.

■ Pandey, B.N., *The Indian Nationalist Movement, 1885–1947: Selected Documents.* New York: St. Martin's Press, 1979.

■ Sarkar, S., *Modern India, 1884–1947.* New York: St. Martin's Press, 1989.

■ Spear, P. And Thapar, R., *A History of India.* 2 vols. Harmondsworth: Penguin, 1965–1966.

■ Stern, R., *Changing India.* Cambridge; Cambridge University Press, 1993.

■ Wolpert, S., *A New History of India.* New York: Oxford University Press, 1997.

Indian Civilization

■ Cohn, B., *An Anthropologist among the Historians and Other Essays.* New Delhi: Oxford University Press, 1988.

■ Naipail, V.S., *India: A Million Mutinies Now.* London: Heinemann; New York: Viking, 1991.

■ Sen, K.M., *Hinduism.* Harmondsworth: Penguin, 1982.

■ Vanima, E. *Ideas and Society in India from the Sixteenth Century to the Eighteenth Century.* New Delhi: Oxford University Press, 1996.

Gandhi's Writings

■ *The Collected Works of Mahatma Gandhi.* 90 vols. New Delhi: Publications Division, Government of India, 1958–1984.

■ Gandhi, M.K., *All Men Are Brothers.* New York: Columbia University Press, 1959.

■ Gandhi, M.K., *An Autobiography: The Stor of My Experiments with Truth.* Boston: Beacon, 1993.

■ Gandhi, M.K., *Gandhi in India in His Own Words.* Ed. M. Green. Hanover, N.H.: University Press of New England, 1987.

■ Gandhi, M.K., *Gandhi on Non-Violence.* Ed T. Merton. New York: New Directions, 1965.

■ Gandhi, M.K., *Hind Swaraj and Other Writings.* Ed. A. Parel. Cambridge: Cambridge University Press, 1997.

■ Gandhi, M.K., *Mahatma Gandhi and Leo Tolstoy Letters.* Ed. B.S. Murthy. Long Beach, Cal.: Long Beach Publications, 1987.

■ Gandhi, M.K., *Selected Political Writings.* Ed. D. Dalton. Indianapolis: Hackett, 1996.

■ Iyer, R. (ed.), *The Moral and Political Writings of Mahatma Gandhi.* 3 vols. Oxford: Clarendon Press, 1986–1987.

■ Mukherjee, R. (Ed.), *The Penguin Gandhi Reader.* Harmondsworth: Penguin, 1993.

Books on Gandhi

■ Bori, P.C. and Sofri, G., *Gandhi e Tolstoj. Un carteggio e dintorni.* Bologna: Il Mulino, 1985.

■ Brown, J.M., *Gandhi's Rise to Power: Indian Politics 1915–1922.* Cambridge: Cambridge University Press, 1974.

■ Dalal, C.B. (ed.), *Gandhi: 1915–1948: A Detailed Chronology.* New Delhi: Gandhi Peace Foundation, 1971.

■ Fox, R., *Gandhian Utopia: Experiments with Culture.* Boston: Beacon, 1989.

■ Mehta, V., *Mahatma Gandhi and His Apostles.* Harmondsworth: Penguin, 1982.

■ Nanda, B.R., *Gandhi and His Critics.* Oxford: Oxford University Press, 1985.
■ Nehru, J., *An Autobiography.* London: Bodley Head, 1989
■ Sofri, G., *Gandhi in Italia.* Bologna: Il Mulino, 1988.
■ Tendulkar, D.G., *Mahatma: Life of Mohandas Karamchand Gandhi.* Pref. By J. Nehru. 8 vols. Delhi: Publications Division, Government of India, 1960–1963.

Fiction
■ Anand, M.R., *Untouchable.* New Delhi: Orient Books, 1970.
■ Chatterji, B.C., *Anandamath.* New Delhi: Vision books, 1992.

■ Cowasjee, S. And Duggal, K.S., eds., *Orphans of the Storm: Stories on the Partition of India.* New Delhi: UBS Publishers, 1995.
■ Mistry, R. *A Fine Balance.* New York: Knopf, 1996.
■ Narayan, R.K., *Waiting for the Mahatma.* New York: Viking, 1958.
■ Roy, A. *The God of Small Things.* New York: Random House, 1997.
■ Rushdie, S., *Midnight's Children.* New York: Vintage, 1995.
■ Sidhwa, B. *Cracking India.* [In the UK: *Ice-Candy-Man.*] Minneapolis: Milkweed, 1991.
■ Tagore, R. *Home and the World.* Harmondsworth: Penguin, 1996.

Chronology

1498	The Portuguese Vasco da Gama lands at Calicut.
1526	Founding of the Moghul Empire by Babur.
1600	Founding of the East India Company in London.
1674	Ceding of Bombay to the British by the Portuguese.
1742–54	Dupleix, head of French possessions, intervenes in numerous conflicts, developing an imperial scheme.
1757	Clive takes back Fort William in Calcutta and wins the battle of Plassey. The British gain control of Bengal.
1773	Warren Hastings is appointed governor general. Hastings grants a monopoly on opium to the East India Company.
1803	British victories over the Marattha. The Moghul emperor comes under British protection.
1829	Abolition of *sati*.
1848–49	Second war against the Sikhs and annexation of Punjab.
1853	Inauguration of the first railway.
1856	Annexation of Oudh. Legalization of marriage for widows.
1857	Sepoy revolt.
1858	Abolition of the East India Company and annexation of India to the British Crown.
1869	Mohandas Karamchand Gandhi is born at Porbandar, in Gujarat.
1877	Queen Victoria is proclaimed Empress of India.
1882	Gandhi married Kasturbai, who is also 13 years old.
1888	Birth of Gandhi and Kasturbai's son, Harilal. Gandhi goes to study law in London; he will remain there until 1891.
1885	Birth of the Indian National Congress.
1893	Gandhi leaves for South Africa.
1896–97	He goes to India, then returns to South Africa with his family. He is attacked on his arrival in Durban.
1899	He organizes an ambulance corps during the Anglo-Boer War.
1901–02	Voyage to India. He participates in a session of Congress.
1903	He founds *Indian Opinion*.
1904	He founds the commune called Phoenix, near Durban. Partition of Bengal.
1904–07	*Swadeshi* movement in Bengal.
1906	Founding of the Muslim League. In South Africa, Gandhi organizes an ambulance corps during the war against the Zulus. He makes a vow of *brahmacharya*. He goes to England to defend the cause of the South African Indians.
1908	Gandhi adopts the term *satyagraha*. For the first time he goes to prison. He encourages the Indians to publicly burn their registration certificates, and illegally enters Transvaal, where he is arrested again.
1909	He goes to England once more. He writes *Hind Swaraj (Indian Home Rule)* and translates Tolstoy's *Letter to a Hindu*.
1910	He sends Tolstoy a copy of *Hind Swaraj* and begins correspondence with the writer.
1912	He abandons European-style clothing.
1913	He guides the great march from Newcastle to Volksrust. He is arrested and condemned several times.
1914	He negotiates with General Smuts. Having reached a compromise, he suspends *satyagraha*. He visits London, after leaving South Africa for good.
1915	He arrives in India. He founds the Satyagraha (later Sabarmati) ashram at Ahmedabad.
1916	He travels throughout India and Burma.
1917	He guides the peasant struggle in Champaran.

1918	He guides the textile workers' struggle in Ahmedabad.
1919	The British issue the Rowlatt acts. Gandhi proclaims and then suspends a *satyagraha* campaign throughout India. He publishes *Navajivan* and *Young India*. Amritsar massacre.
1920	Gandhi decides to wear *khadi* for the rest of his life. He becomes the unrivalled leader of Congress, which he persuades to support nonviolent means in the struggle in favor of the Caliphate and home rule.
1921	Gandhi vows to spin cotton each day. He begins mass *satyagraha*.
1922	After the violence at Chauri Chaura, he stops the non-cooperation movement. He is arrested and sentenced to six years in prison.
1924	Gandhi is released from prison. He fasts in favor of unity between Hindus and Muslims.
1925	He begins writing his autobiography.
1930	Birth of the concept of a separate Muslim state. Salt march. New civil disobedience movements (1930–1931 and 1932–1933).
1931	Gandhi-Irwin Pact. He goes to London and participates in the Round Table Conference. On his return he visits Romain Rolland in Switzerland, and stops in Italy.
1932	He is arrested and fasts against separate electorates for untouchables.
1933	He founds the journal *Harijan*. He leaves and re-enters prison.
1934	He escapes an assassination attempt.
1935	Government of India Act.
1936	He moves to Sevagram, near Wardha.
1937	After the electoral victory, formation of provincial Congress governments.
1940	The Muslim League adopts a resolution on Pakistan. Gandhi starts a limited campaign of civil disobedience against the forced participation of India in the war.
1942	Gandhi launches the *Quit India* movement. He is arrested and imprisoned in the villa of the Aga Khan at Pune.
1944	Death of Kasturbai. Gandhi is released. Start of talks with Jinnah.
1946	Riots break out between the religious communities. Gandhi participates in talks on the future of India. He escapes another terrorist attack. He journeys on foot around Bengal, which has been torn by violence between Hindus and Muslims.
1947	Lord Mountbatten, the last viceroy, arrives in India. Gandhi strenuously opposes the partition of India. In August, India and Pakistan become independent. Nehru is Prime Minister of India. Gandhi fasts against Hindu-Muslim violence.
1947– 48	Massacres in Punjab and exodus of peoples. On January 30 Gandhi is killed. Death of Jinnah. First conflict between India and Pakistan over Kashmir.
1955	Nehru participates in the movement of non-aligned countries, at Bandung.
1959	Chinese occupation of Tibet and flight of the Dalai Lama to India. Border conflict.
1962	War between India and China.
1964	Death of Nehru. He is succeeded by L.B. Shastri.
1965	War with Pakistan.
1966	Indira Gandhi becomes premier.
1971	War with Pakistan in support of Bangladesh's secession.Indira Gandhi proclaims the
1975	"state of emergency" and reduces the opposition to silence.
1977	Electoral defeat of Indira Gandhi and Congress by Janata coalition. Moraji Desai forms the government.
1979	Indira Gandhi wins the elections and returns to govern the following year.
1984	The army attacks the Golden Temple at Amritsar. Indira Gandhi is assassinated by two Sikhs. Rajiv Gandhi succeeds her.
1991	Assassination of Rajiv Gandhi.
1996	Electoral success of Hindu nationalists. Center-left government headed by H.D. Deve Gowda.
1998	Election of Hindu nationalist government of the BJP party. India conducts five nuclear tests.

Index of names

The Traveller's History Series

A Traveller's History of the Caribbean	$14.95/£8.99 pb
A Traveller's History of China	$14.95/£8.99 pb
A Traveller's History of England	$14.95/£8.99 pb
A Traveller's History of France	$14.95/£8.99 pb
A Traveller's History of Greece	$14.95/£7.95 pb
A Traveller's History of India	$14.95/£8.99 pb
A Traveller's History of Ireland	$14.95/£7.95 pb
A Traveller's History of Italy	$14.95/£8.99 pb
A Traveller's History of Japan	$14.95/£8.99 pb
A Traveller's History of London	$14.95/£8.99 pb
A Traveller's History of North Africa	$14.95/£8.99 pb
A Traveller's History of Paris	$14.95/£8.99 pb
A Traveller's History of Russia	$14.95/£7.95 pb
A Traveller's History of Scotland	$14.95/£8.99 pb
A Traveller's History of Spain	$14.95/£8.99 pb
A Traveller's History of Turkey	$14.95/£8.99 pb

Available at good bookshops everywhere
We encourage you to support your local bookseller

To order or request a full list of titles
please contact us at one of the addresses listed below:

In the US:
Interlink Publishing
Group Inc.
46 Crosby Street
Northampton, MA 01060
Tel: 800-238-LINK/Fax: 413-582-7057
e-mail: interpg@aol.com

In the UK:
Windrush Press Ltd.
Little Window, High Street
Moreton-in-Marsh
Gloucestershire GL56 0LL
Tel: 01608 652012/Fax 01608 652125
email: windrush@netcomuk.co.uk